Who Knew?

<u>A Memoir</u>

By: Sann Curlred

For interviews or any inquiries pertaining to the content of this publication, contact the author via email:

sannredd4@gmail.com

Edited, Formatted, and Published via *iWrite4orU*:

www.iWrite4orU.com

Cover Designed by: Janelle Jones

Print ISBN: 978-0-9998842-9-4

Library of Congress Control Number: 2021914256

Printed in the United States of America

ACKNOWLEDGMENTS

To my husband, for his encouragement and commitment to my writing debut.

To my daughter, for helping with the editing process.

To my sister, for agreeing to read my story just before it went to press and giving me her feedback.

To my surviving brothers and sisters, who allowed me to intertwine their lives with mine as I tell our story.

To my children, for their unquestioning belief and devotion to me and this project.

To my grandchildren, who helped with technology.

To my great granddaughter, a bright spot of so much joy in my life.

To both my parents, for making me the woman I am today.

To my friends, for their insistent encouragement to keep writing.

To constituents of Progressive Mission and Education Baptist State Convention of Florida, Inc., who heard part of my story and encouraged me, immensely.

To Lakeland Library Writers group, for lessons presented and encouraging words for completion of this manuscript.

Special Gratitude to my mentor, Editor/Publisher, Liltera R. Williams, for taking on my project to share my story as a novice writer; for taking a rough manuscript and helping to create a literary work.

To my childhood friend, for taking on the daunting task of drafting the book cover without having read the book first.

To my Mama, the strongest woman I ever knew, who provided the inspiration for this story.

To military wives and families everywhere, who read my story and can move on to write their own story with the happy endings they anticipate. Your strength and dedication to your spouse is appreciated. Your military person is risking life for a patriotic cause. He/she may not know how to express that to you. You have permission to ask for what you need.

To children of military personnel, who need the love and understanding of parents who are frequently absent: be strong, respectful, and voice your concerns, with love.

To military personnel, thank you for your service to our country. Your duty to country is commendable. Honor and respect is also due to the spouse who supports you in that endeavor.

PROLOGUE

In 1963, the year I turned fourteen and entered high school, integration began for me. I attended the white school, previously, just for the privileged, the white privileged. That year, I realized all things are not always as they seem. For reasons I cannot remember, my mother walked down the hallway of my new school. For the first time ever, I saw my mother as the white privileged may have seen her. I was embarrassed that she was there in her old, frayed winter wool coat and rocked-over, low-heeled shoes. She walked very slowly, probably tired out from the mile-long walk from home to the school. Her all-too-familiar flowered headscarf was tied neatly under her chin. Her African-American, Indian, and Caucasian heritage gave her the look of someone who could have been a beautiful woman in another situation, in other times. Her sunken, bronzed cheeks glowed from being in the harsh, cold temperatures outside.

"Why is she here" I wondered. *"Had I done something wrong?"*

I did not want her to see me. I did not want to talk to her, so I stayed behind her. We did not speak or otherwise acknowledge each other. I assumed that she was there for me. But why? And why was she wearing those awful old shoes?

I was embarrassed because I thought that I reflected her: green, misplaced, misfit, afraid of the new environment. Watching her as she walked down those halls reinforced my insecurities. My teenage mind wanted to "wish her out" of there before anyone else saw her.

I then grew ashamed of my embarrassment. In my heart, I asked Mama to forgive me. For the remainder of her life, I tried to make it up to her. Maybe I am still trying. She said on numerous occasions that she wanted to write a book, a story about her life, and wanted others to know about the struggles she experienced; about the kind of life that she had lived; how she had made a difference in the lives of others. However, we did not write that book. We could never seem to find the time to make it happen. Therefore, as I write my story, I also write this for Mama. I know that she would forgive my adolescent thoughts, as I try to forgive myself. I also cannot write a story about myself and my memories without including my family and the people who have made an impact in my life.

As John Donne said, "No man is an island, entire of itself." Nothing happens without it happening to those around me.

And, as the African proverb states, "It takes a village to raise a child."

I was fortunate to have helpful, encouraging, and generous people in my village. This is my tribute to my mother and to the kind, generous, sparkling, and hardworking, God-fearing person that she was.

Ecclesiastes 3:1,15

New King James Version (The Open Bible)

"To everything there is a season, A time for every purpose
under heaven: (3:1)
That which is has already been,
and what is to be has already been:
And God requires an account of what is past." (3:15)

INTRODUCTION

This story tells how two lives were woven intricately together. Mama's story merges with mine, as an extremely bashful young girl in an economically depressed family, who lived an extraordinary life. I hesitate to say that mine was a dysfunctional family because I do not like that word; I think that we were more of a broken family trying to put ourselves back together while at the same time keeping all our secrets hidden.

I am a woman, a Black woman, a single mother, a military wife, a cancer survivor, and a professional who was successful in my career choices. I was abused through physical and mental endeavors in my family and suffered the indignation of racism and discrimination as an accepted way of life. I realized early that my family and I were poor, then came to know that there are shades of poverty and that in any shade, it is a difficult thing to overcome. Being married has its own set of issues, as well, and being married to a soldier brought added stress to the relationship. I had to learn in battling two different cancers, one being terminal, that life is precious and fleeting. I write my story to encourage all women to never give up hope because in the end, the struggle is worth it. My life journey would encounter familial abuse, personal disregard, racism, discrimination, and discontent with a projected limited life in a small town. My heart and my head wanted more.

My journey led me to fight for life in more ways than one. The wretchedness of a rare, chronic cancer and a multitude of other chronic illnesses invaded my body as I fought to hold my young family, career, and marriage together while traveling as a military wife. It was under these conditions, that I learned to survive. Memories flood my consciousness as I relive parts of my life in this season, as I travel back into my past. Who knew what I would find in one season of my life as I anticipated the next?

Note to Readers: In an effort not to offend, the term 'Colored' historically refers to people who are not "white". Black people have been called many things. Colored was the term used in the United States instead of African, during the Civil Rights movement of the 50-60s. It was a derogatory term that was utilized during the Jim Crow era. Its usage declined from 1920 until 1966. By the 1950s, the dominant name was Negro. Colored was used simultaneously with Negro from 1920 to 1966. Colored was not a preference after that time. Negro was used until 1974, when the Black Power movement emerged with the term Black. President Obama signed into law as official names African American and Asian American in 2010. Black/African American was the language used on official forms. When I was very young, I was called "Colored". Around age twelve, I was called "Negro", until the latter part of the 60s, when I was Black. I have tried to be true to what was going on in my environment. Now, I am Black or African American. But, I know I am more than that, with my Indian and European blood, which is hard to prove. Just call me Black. I am proud to be Black and the terms African American and Black are used interchangeably in today's America.

Chapter 1

TAKING A LOOK BACK

A Class Reunion

Friends come and go, but sometimes there is a friend who stays in touch and keeps the relationship intact. Such was the nature of the friendship between Carol and me. We were friends before starting school in grade one. We lost contact for several years but managed to meet in our hometown of Cadiz, Kentucky, to refresh and revive our relationship. Both our parents lived in Cadiz, so it was easy to make the initial connection. My daughter and her friend's daughter were going to be leaving home for college.

We were on a tour evaluating prospective schools for them. It was coincidence, or fate, that we both were there at the same time. Carol mentioned that she had gotten an invitation to the 1967 graduating high school class of Trigg County High School's fiftieth class reunion.

"We should go," I insisted, telling our children how much fun the last one had been. I remembered the last one. I did not think it was fun, particularly. That had been after we had been out of school forty-five years. I had not seen my former classmates prior to that reunion.

As I recalled the meeting, I remembered that our white classmates did not remember us. They knew our names but confused our faces. Carol and I had been friends in high school and were often seen together. I guess it was not surprising that they mixed us up after so many years. Add that to the fact that both of us had moved away and made our homes elsewhere.

Carol convinced me to go to our fiftieth reunion. She lived in New York and I lived in Florida. I was a reluctant participant, as my memories were mostly unpleasant and infuriating. I had not enjoyed high school. But, I let her talk me into going. We decided to meet up when we got to Cadiz and go to the affair together. I would rent a cabin at Barkley Lodge and we would stay together for the weekend event. When we got there, things were mostly good. We were having a good time. Carol and I flew into the airport in Nashville, Tennessee. We had a brief time together before we moved on to the Friday night event. We participated in the Meet and Greet activity at Lake Barkley State Park, a place where I worked in the kitchen one summer while I was in college. I knew the ins and outs of the place. Nothing had changed.

The attendance of the Black constituents of the class of 1967 was not well represented. There could have been, according to my estimation, ten to twelve instead of the three who showed up. When I was in high school, I felt like I was out of place. There seemed to have been an undercurrent of uncertainty. To me, it was always there.

Did they not want me there? Did I not want to be there? Was I out of my league in my homemade clothes? Did the teachers there try to intentionally isolate me?

Class reunion August 2017 felt exactly like Integration Day in 1963. On Saturday, night of the reunion, following a delicious buffet meal, we were socializing and catching up with each other on things that had happened over the last fifty years. One of the classmates, part of the program committee, gave a very lengthy presentation about the history of education in Trigg County and how they honor the teachers they had. Black children were completely excluded. It was as if we never attended school there or anywhere.

Our Black teachers were not given a place of honor in the presentation. The presenter took us exactly to the point where integration was mandated and, there, he stopped the scenario. My aunts had been teaching during that time. It was so infuriating to be so arrogantly bypassed. It totally excluded the education of Black students and the contributions of Black teachers in the county.

I got angry and promised myself to not go to that reunion and subject myself all over again to the feelings of dismissal and having no place in that school life.

Perhaps things did change, depending on the perspective. Perhaps, I expected more change so that I could be included. My white classmate was speaking about what he knew but he did not have the right to make me feel invisible. As I compare the place my parents and grandparents had come from, I can see a major difference in our lives. I will tell my story from that perspective. The experiences that they likely had in their lives with biases, racism, discrimination, and abuse among hard times could have been the same that I experienced.

<u>The Move</u>

Excitement was palpable as seven children waited anxiously to get going on moving day in 1949. I can only imagine the jubilation they felt.

Mama was pregnant. I would be the first to be born in Trigg County, Kentucky. Outdated farm equipment, including a plow, disc, hole diggers, rakes, shovels, and dollies had already been moved to Cadiz. Their lonely old house, weathered and devoid of paint, sitting on the hilltop amid eighteen acres of tall grass and carefully cultivated fields of corn and burley tobacco, was cleaned. A half-century-old iron bed frame, a scratched and scarred dresser, with its oval mirror, peeling along its beveled edges, had been packed. That old dresser was a valuable and solitary heirloom left to Mama, a keepsake from mother to daughter, precious to Mama. Her mother had passed away when she was seven years old. This dresser was all she had left of her; a treasure.

"This is my gift from me to you. Take care of it," she had told Mama. Years later, Mama used these same words when she gave it to me. I passed it on to my daughter when she set up housekeeping with her family. I told her the story of where it had come from. Mama would have wanted it to be kept in the family.

The kitchen was bare now, as pots, dented pans, chipped dishes, and dishrags made from linen or cotton flour sacks were packed into wooden crates. Black cast iron skillets, the round metal bathing tub, washing machine, with its crank for squeezing water out of clothes and the big black iron pot used for making soap, and used during hog-killings, were on the sidelines to be packed on the next load. A solitary cow, several pigs, chickens, and roosters would be moved later, according to my then eleven-year-old sister, Neta.

Mooing, cackling, and animals oinking created a cacophony of pandemonium. Daddy and Mama were making their move of a lifetime. Both of them had been born on the ridge. Mama had given birth to seven of her children here. They were moving the family and working farm from Ditney Ridge to a location on the border of Kentucky and Tennessee called Trigg County, Kentucky. They had saved their money and purchased a tract of six acres of land in the southwest corner of Kentucky for four-hundred dollars. They were moving to an under-developed part of town where only colored people lived.

Hopefully, this move would elevate their status in society and improve living conditions. This was part of my heritage. I grew up on the borderline of the North and South in rural Kentucky, a state with a dubious 1950's history. We did not live in the Appalachian Mountains, the imagery that is often associated with Kentucky. Coal was mined from those mountains. Coal mining was the way of life there. It was their livelihood. People who lived there were touted as being very poor, barely managing to scrape an existence from the land. Some have even called it hillbilly country—a derogatory name, inferring being slow-witted, poor, and uneducated.

New acquaintances often ask me, "Where are you from?"

When I reply that I am a Kentuckian, they respond with disbelief: "You don't look or sound like a hillbilly?"

At that point, I feel compelled to explain the different parts of Kentucky and their peculiarities. Even though our domiciles were hundreds of miles apart, there were some things that we had in common with our Appalachian counterparts. The state is called the bluegrass state due to the characteristic emerald-green tint found on the grass in many parts of the state. My part of Kentucky, Cadiz, a small town in a rural area, is closer to the state of Illinois.

This grass flourishes in many parts of the state, in its state parks and horse pastures across the eastern part of the state. Another thing that both parts of the state have in common happened during the Great Depression, in the 1930s and 1940s.

Unemployment was rampant, and the construction of new projects plummeted. Many parts of Kentucky did not recuperate from this setback. The Appalachian Mountain area and the coal mining industry dominate the list of the worst places to live in the United States, even now, according to the

Courier Journal Newspaper, Louisville KY: Samuel Stebbins and Michael Sauter: "10 Worst Places to Live", March 13, 2019. Additionally, Kentucky is the fifth poorest state in the nation. This assessment is based on poverty level, income of less than $30,000 annually, life expectancy at birth, and the percentage of individuals having obtained a Bachelor of Science degree.

Although there are numerous state parks, with rivers and lakes and other recreational areas like resorts and boating and fishing establishments, the state still has not come out of its depression. Houses that were built during this period of history were clapboard houses without insulation in the walls, set up on blocks to have root cellar space underneath for storing vegetables and fruits that were grown and harvested at the end of their growing season. Their method of heating these houses was with a potbelly stove or fireplaces that burned either coal or wood. Houses were small and families were large.

Houses were hot during summertime and freezing cold in wintertime. The most you had for keeping houses cool in summer was an electrical box window fan. Portable window air conditioners would come later. This is what I knew about; the area where teachers were desperately needed. One of the county school systems offered me a job in these mountains, to teach for two years and obtain forgiveness of my student loan. These are the conditions my family moved into.

Kentucky had well-defined weather seasons. In early spring of each year, fields were plowed in readiness for planting seeds of vegetables. Vegetables were grown for our food. I loved this time of year. My brothers, youngest sister and I got up early in the mornings. We raced to see who could make their bed and get to breakfast the fastest. That done, we could get started on chores. Once our chores were completed, we played and ran, chased each other and dropped the variety of seeds in the dirt, starting the planting season.

There would be plenty of green pole beans, snap peas, carrots, tomatoes, potatoes, and corn. Summertime was harvest time. During the fall season, root vegetables were harvested and put in the cellar. Sorghum, made from sugar cane, was cooked during the hog-killing season. Pork, from the pigs, was processed and stored in the smoke house. Tobacco beds were planted in spring. When the plants were big enough, they would be put in the ground for the annual crop. Daddy planted his crop and also worked on a white man's property as a sharecropper. Our move to Cadiz had been a step up. We hoped that our quality of life would improve so we would no longer be the country bumpkin cousins.

My family's expectations were high as we moved into the 1950's. Future acts unfolded, unlike past experiences, but with many of the same kinds of things experienced in the past. My large family would be no strangers to hard times as we worked hard to be successful in the new home.

Chapter 2

FAMILY LIFE

Our House

Our new home was adjacent to Aunt Marie's house. Both houses were set in a depressed area that extended from the highway down into our yard. It can be likened to living in a valley. When it rained, water gushed down the incline into the yard creating a water-lodged yard. Our house stood on blocks and the water ran underneath to a drainage ditch behind the house. Rumor was that the house had been used as a chicken coop by a previous owner. Daddy and my brothers worked to make it a livable home.

The differences in our house and Aunt Marie's house summed up the way I felt about the difference is in our lives. In those days, our house was weathered and unpainted, with linoleum rugs on the floors. We had an outhouse to take care of private toilet needs. Originally, there were four rooms in our house. The two front rooms each had two glass-paned windows. Therefore, each room had one window on each of the outside walls. Our house was heated with coal burning stoves. Both bedrooms were on the front side of the house. One of them doubled as a living or sitting room.

One of the rooms on the back side was a bedroom for our parents, which contained a half bed and a double size bed. Sleeping arrangements were simple. Both front bedrooms had full size beds so two siblings slept in each four beds. My youngest sibling slept in the half-bed. Another room in our four-room house was the kitchen; this room contained a large table. It was very versatile, used for meal preparation, serving meals and was a general work area and congregating area. There was no insulation in the walls or ceilings. Winters were harsh. The house was heated with a coal-burning stove in the front room and often smelled of coal and kerosene. It might also smell like fried chicken or fish or baked pastries. Something was always cooking because somebody was always hungry. There were a lot of mouths to feed.

The kitchen stove was a wood burning stove. During the harvest and canning season, the house had the pungent smell of pickles and vinegar or fresh fruit. Our house was always spotless. Mama took pride in making sure everything was always clean: windows were washed, floor boards were scrubbed, furniture was waxed and dusted regularly, and floors were spotless.

Daddy's sister, Marie, lived in the house next door with her husband and two sons. There was a difference in our family size and activity. Our houses, though next door to each other, were vastly different. Even though we had a close relationship and got along well, I thought, at the time, there was always an undercurrent of discontent and being too young to discriminate, thought that we were one big happy family.

Aunt Marie's house was painted white with blue-green trim around the windows. It had shiny hardwood floors inside and a shiny upright piano sat on top of those floors in the dining room. The adjacent room was the living room with a sofa, chair, end tables with lamps and a black and white television sat in one corner. Neither house was built with hallways. One room opened into another room, but there was extra room at the back. Aunt Marie's house was heated electrically. When Mama would let us go to her house, it smelled like flowers. Unlike our house, which smelled like whatever was cooking at the time. Even though we were all family living next door to each other, I felt like we were inferior. Daddy's sisters were educated and presented themselves as professionals in the community. His brothers had moved away to work in industrial jobs in the city. I knew there was something better than what I could see in my small part of the world. I got a little peek at what I could aspire to be by watching my aunts and older siblings.

A Full House

Even though there were so many of us in our house, Mama loved us all. She hugged and kissed us and treated each one special. She was jovial and helpful in the neighborhood. Mama wanted all her children to receive an education. She had not finished high school and expressed regret that she had not done so.

My eldest brother, Nat, attended high school but did not graduate. He joined the U.S. Army as a teenager and fought in the Korean War. After getting out of the army, Nat moved to Indianapolis, Indiana, and worked in the construction industry. He married Lorine. They had one son, Lee.

Neta, my oldest sister, attended and graduated from Attucks High School, in Hopkinsville. She went on to attend college at Kentucky State College in Frankfort and started her degree, but went on to work as a nanny in New York. Neta gave birth to her first child shortly after leaving college, got her nursing credentials later and worked in the nursing field for the remainder of her working career. She relocated to north Florida and continues to live there. She married David, had one daughter, Cynthia, and three boys, Mario, Curtis, and Kevin.

My brother Lewis, or Buster, was the one who worked around the farm and around the house. He was always helpful. There was an accident when he was a child that resulted in his being blind in one eye. I never really understood how the accident happened, but there were a few different stories. Some say the boys were playing a game and something hit Buster in the eye. So, he always had one crazy looking eye. Others say it was an accident with a BB gun while the boys were playing. I also heard it involved a spring on the screen door that broke loose and hit him in the eye. No one ever explained why his eye did not get fixed. Buster later moved to Indianapolis where he worked for many years. He had one son, Greg. Buster married Barbara and their marriage lasted a few years. Buster passed away with cancer many years later.

We called my brother Tommie, "Ballie," but he liked to be known as "The Professor". When he graduated high school, one of the teachers at Attucks suggested he attend Kentucky State College.

Ballie was at home during summer breaks, so he helped with the farm work. He graduated with a bachelor's degree in biology, moved to Indianapolis, and began his teaching career. He worked as a high school teacher and Assistant Principal at Broad Ripple High School. He earned his Master's and Specialist degrees at Ball State University. Ballie married Effie, a hometown young lady. They had four children: Chris, Yolanda, Mark, and Tom Junior. He later retired from that system and continued to live near Indianapolis until he passed away a few days before his eightieth birthday.

Jean was christened Cora Jean but was favored with Jean. She was born after two boys and before two boys. All births were single births. I always thought she was the most lovable person. She took me on as her special project. After she graduated from Attucks, she got a job working at the local clothing manufacturing company, Elk Brand. She wanted to be a nurse, but Daddy said he was not sending anymore girls to college. He told her no and she accepted it. She married a local young man, Quincy, and they had four children: Quintina, Stacey, Stefan, and Michelle.

When Jean had her own house, I was there frequently. She lived and worked in Cadiz her whole life. She was the caregiver for Mama and Daddy as they got older and needed help to care for themselves.

Junior, born sixth, did not live beyond infancy.

The next child to be born was Grady. He was part of the younger set of siblings, which included my younger brother, Ollie; sister, Zora; and me. Grady was born with a birth defect that affected his eyes, and he had unusual facial features. I know there was a name for what he had but I never knew what it was called. Instead, Ollie and I gave him a nickname that we could only use out of Mama's earshot. We called him "Popeye" because his eyes were too big for his face. He had major vision issues and was declared legally blind by the age of twelve. There were no systems in place for colored children with special needs in the standard school system, so he struggled.

When Grady was fourteen, Mama, Daddy, his teachers, and a social worker made the decision to send him to the Kentucky School for the Blind in Louisville from middle school through high school to get the help that he needed for his education. I felt miserable that he had to go away.

I was despondent for a while, after he left. I missed my playmate and confidant, but we made the adjustment and communicated by writing letters to each other. Sometimes, my family would pack up our 1951 Ford and drive the 200 miles to visit him. Over the years, Grady learned to manipulate the transportation system and would ride the bus home for holidays; he never lived with us again. Grady had to learn to fit in at the school because he had always lived in the sighted world, but now had to live as a severely impaired sighted person in a sight-less environment. He stayed there and earned his high school diploma. We were so proud of him. After his graduation, he took a job at the school and stayed in Louisville.

Grady was a quiet, generous person, and I soon regretted that I had participated in the childhood meanness of name-calling. He had a strong faith in God and practiced his faith. I visited him a few times when I was in college since we were only about sixty miles apart. I would have thought that he resented the rest of us because he had to leave the family. But he did not. Instead, he relished the opportunity to live in his new environment. I loved to talk to him about everything. He was a very accessible young man, who just seemed to know what to do and when to do it. Once when I was visiting Grady in Louisville, he and I went shopping to buy a new coat for me. This was a big deal. I had only worn hand-me-downs.

I was so excited as we shopped. He bought my first new coat; it was a double-breasted, A-line, and brilliant reddish-orange color. It was flashy and more than just a little over the top. Later, I realized this was probably the worst choice for everyday winter-time wear.

At first, believe it or not, it was sort of embarrassing wearing it, because it stood out so much. However, I had no choice. It was my only coat, so I decided to flaunt it, adding a long black knitted scarf that wrapped around my neck a few times. I saw myself as a trendsetter. I did learn a valuable lesson, though. If I must spend the money, then I should get what I want but shop wisely. Grady's buying that orange coat for me started a pattern that would continue through my adult life—the thrill of buying expensive things, but knowing when to indulge, and when to hold my peace.

Being child number eight, my place in the clan earned me no special privileges. I had inherited the wide space between my two front teeth from Daddy, so I became the little gap-toothed girl. Grady and Ollie nicknamed me Gabby. I fell on my face and broke the edge off one of those front teeth. By the time I was a teenager, the space between my teeth had gotten bigger because I was always unconsciously poking my tongue through it. That did not help my self-esteem at school. I did not know, as a child, that my tooth could have had a cap or crown placed on it. Even if I did know, there was no money in our household for such things. There were no regular dental or medical checkups. If you had a cavity, you told Mama when it started to hurt. A trip to the local dentist was to have it extracted. I smiled less and less. By brothers teased me and gave me a new nickname, "Buckteeth". I wished they had fixed my teeth. My self-esteem suffered.

Oliver, dubbed Ollie, was my best friend. We were born eighteen months apart. He and I did everything together. He was a vital part of our community play group. In high school, he was an avid long-distance runner. He finished high school at Trigg County High, one year after I did, and was drafted into the U. S. Army. Soon after his Basic Trainings, he was sent to Vietnam where he fought in that war. I worried for him, because so many young men did not return. I wrote letters to him and prayed for him. We stayed in touch. Ollie did come home. He married Margaret and they had three girls: Tenesha, Shanel, and Rona.

Zora, our youngest sibling, born late in Mama's life, six years younger than I, garnished more privileges and new things like store-bought clothing. By the time she was an adolescent, our older siblings contributed to the family income or outright made purchases for the household. After college, Zora married Kent, a soldier, and they had two children, Jason and Jamie. Each child in the family looked out for each other's safety. Our youngest sister went to Eastern Kentucky University in Richmond, Kentucky, graduating with a degree in Interpersonal Communications. Later, she married Ron. She also earned her Master's degree while working as an educator in the public school system in Florida. She loved helping others and became a minister after attending seminary schools. Mama had plans for each of her eight remaining children. Each one had their own journey to make. Mine would lead me to places I had only read and dreamed about.

High school students were bussed to Attucks, before integration, to the Negro high school, which was twenty miles away in Hopkinsville. That is where my older brothers and sisters went. Neta, my oldest sister told me they went there in grades eleven and twelve. They got up early to catch the bus that would take them to their studies. Mama truly believed that education and a positive attitude, along with hard work, would ensure her children a successful future. All the children finished high school, except Nat. Mama wanted so much more for her children, so she pushed us, encouraging us to be successful.

She said many times, "I wanted to be a nurse when I grew up." She left school after eleventh grade, got married and started a family. Both my parents could read and write and take care of their business.

Mama and Daddy had a total of ten children. As is often true in large families, older siblings leave the nest before some of the younger ones are born. My oldest sister, Neta, was almost twelve when I was born. Nat left home at age sixteen. My mama loved helping others and practically raised her friend Vesta's children. One or more of her children was frequently at our house. Later, Mama and Daddy took in Neta's children for a time to help with raising them. My first child lived with Mama and Daddy the first year of his life. Being part of a large family cemented the idea that loving families help each other through tough times.

Chapter 3

THE NEIGHBORHOOD

The Happiness of Childhood

This part of my life was a happy, carefree time, having fun and playing among family and the neighborhood children. Back then, being happy meant spending time with friends and family, even if it was a large one like ours. As I got older, the family demographics changed. As I started my journey, it would change again and again. Our family dynamic was not the only change. Physical changes happened slowly in our part of town. There were no sidewalks, running water or sewage lines running through our neighborhood. That would come a few years later, when the town had a vested interest in our part of town.

The Colored part of town concentrated in an area that was less than one mile in either direction. A major roadway ran through the center of it. Our house sat along the major road. When I was growing up, there were more than fifty children who rallied around my age. There was usually someone to play with. Across the street neighbors' kids included: Teresa, Jerry, Ronnie, and their other four younger siblings. Sonny, from down the street, played with us a lot. Some of Ms. Vesta's children, George or Loretta, were frequently there. Sometimes, Cheyenne, Vonnie and Shelia, from further down the road, across the road, joined the playing.

We made up games, including many kinds of variations of hide-and-seek. There were plenty of places to hide. Daddy gave us a used rope and helped to make a swing, which looped over a strong tree limb and attached an old, discarded car tire. We jumped rope, including Double Dutch and made-up games. The girls made mudpies and cooked outside in the yard; pretend cooking, that is. We drew hopscotch diagrams in the dirt with a stick and played hopscotch until we were too tired to hop. Sometimes, we played kick the can or softball using a stick for a bat, provided someone had a bat and a ball. We played together at each other's houses and yards. An empty field meant we could play ball. There were two fields right in the neighborhood. One was in our yard.

Mama was a great cook and kept us supplied with an abundance of homemade cookies, as we played. She would put them in a straw basket and leave them for us to munch on. We ate them quickly, though, getting drinks of water from the bucket sitting next to the cistern. The cookies, she called Tea Cakes, were a bit larger than a two-and-a-half-inch biscuit, concocted quickly using flour, lard, a little sugar, milk, and a little bit of vanilla flavoring. These economically prepared cookies were baked to golden-brown perfection in our wood-burning oven. There was plenty for everybody. We had more playmates on the days when Mama made cookies for us.

There was an orchard, which meant plenty of trees to climb and plenty of fresh fruit in the summertime. We feasted on apples, peaches, and pears. One afternoon, as I sat high up in a large, fully-grown apple tree, munching on an apple, I fell. I did not weigh enough to fall all the way to the ground, so I was caught up by crisscrossed branches. The branches broke my fall and I just hung there. When I saw that I was bleeding, I quickly climbed down from the tree.

I ran, crying, straight to Mama begging her, "Mama! I am bleeding. It hurts so bad. Will you make it stop?"

My leg was bleeding rather profusely. I knew she would make me feel better.

"Girl, what have you done now?" she said as she patiently examined the wound and cleaned it.

Then, she wrapped it with a slice of bacon and covered it with a clean white cloth (no Band-Aids for us). I did not understand the science behind that ritual, but the wound healed, and I was fine. However, I still have a faint scar on my left thigh where the branch caught me and dug into my leg. Sometimes, I would sit high up in a fruit tree and read to my heart's content, which is what I was doing that day. I continued to use those trees as my favorite reading spots and occasional hiding places.

There was not much to do in the small town, except maybe go to the library. I discovered the public library, downtown, at an early age. I could go there with an older brother or sister. We all had library cards. Books could also be borrowed from school. I developed a literary sense. I loved words. I loved to read and would read writings by Negro authors, as well as white writers. In those days, it did not matter to me. I read for hours. One of my favorite books included *Gone with the Wind*, by Margaret Mitchell. I read it when I was ten years old. I had long lists of words to study. Many of my favorite books were of historical fiction and works done by Negro authors, like James Baldwin's "Black Like Me".

By reading, I could project myself any place at any time and into any culture; it was my escape. I wanted to see some of those places I read about and do some of the things that the people in my books did. The problem was how? I had no money; I had no means of transportation. The only thing

I had was my imagination. I was a good student and figured education may be a way out.

Early School Days

In the beginning, at Dunbar school, one teacher taught all the students in one grade for neighborhood Colored children. Some children were bussed in from around the county, but I walked 500 feet every day because the school was located on the property right next to our house. Three of the elementary teachers were my aunts, my father's sisters. Bad behavior was not tolerated and was met with punishment with a strap. Any misbehaving child would have to stand in front of the whole class with their hand held out in front, palm facing up, to receive a slap on the palm of their hand, administered by the teacher with the strap.

Most students were determined not to cry, but invariably tears, unaccompanied by sounds, ran down the face. I made sure not to have infractions to avoid punishment. Had I gotten the strap, I would have gotten punished again, possibly with a switch, from my parents, when I got home. A switch was simply a small branch torn from a tree. Some parents got creative and twisted two or three branches (more like twigs) or allowed a misbehaving child to select it.

Mama, listening to what had happened at school, said, "Go on outside and get a switch."

There was an art to choosing one: not too thin or I would have to choose another one, but not too thick because it would be too painful with each strike. If the chosen switch was too small, Mama would go get another one that was more to her liking. Mama handed down most of the punishments.

During this time and later, I stayed nights with Aunt Cora, who was unmarried and lived just down the street from us. She was a teacher at Dunbar, so we walked to school together every morning. I guessed that she was afraid to stay alone in her house at night, for some reason.

During the time I lived with my Aunt Cora, she packed a bag lunch for me every day. I sat in my classroom and ate my lunch with students who were bussed in. It would have taken me about a half a minute to walk home for lunch, but Aunt Cora always insisted. She paid for me to have a three cents bottle of milk every day, and every day, I poured the milk out the window and prayed I would not get caught wasting her money. I also prayed that Mama did not find out. I did not like milk at all. That was more than likely because I had to drink fresh milk from our lone cow when I was very young, but blessings sometimes show up in unusual ways. At least I did not have to milk the cow.

Students brought lunch to school or walked to their homes for lunch. There were some enterprising Colored men who had business establishments in the neighborhood. Mr. Jack sold candy and sodas at his joint next to the school. He mostly sold stuff off his truck. He was called The Junk Man. Mr. Henry's joint was just across the street. He had food, candy, cigarettes, pop, and so forth, plus he had a jukebox so on weekends and evenings it was the local hangout where everybody went to dance and socialize. I could only go there with direction from my parents.

Mama would sometimes tell me to go get a bottle of Pepsi from Mr. Henry's. She gave me a nickel to pay for it. Then she watched me from the shelter of our porch, until I came back with her Pepsi. She would sit on the front porch and drink it after giving each one of the children, who were standing around wanting a drink a "swallow".

Seemingly, she did not get much of that drink after sharing, but she always shared and enjoyed what was left of the drink, as she relaxed. As we grew older, we stopped asking for a share of that drink, probably realizing that this was something that Mama needed just for herself.

Mama sent us to school, but she was too busy to supervise our learning. Subjects of reading, writing, arithmetic, science, science and other subjects were monitored by older siblings. A health class would have been the appropriate class for learning about body parts and their functions. However, the concept of teaching sex education was avoided. Parents did not discuss it, and it was certainly not mentioned in our house. The stork still brought babies.

Consequently, my elementary days were filled with secrets that nobody knew about. My brothers, Grady and Ollie, and friends in the neighborhood played "show and tell" games and discussed the differences in our anatomy. Jean told me that it was not a good thing to play those kinds of games with the boys. Nobody told me why. I would have to learn later. When I got older, Jean explained "the facts of life" to me, while I gawked in embarrassment.

There were no lessons in school about body parts and how they related to each other. We were not taught about where babies came from or how they were made or the reproductive process. Many things, though, were taught in our "separate but equal" neighborhood schools. Sex education was not one of them. We learned from each other on the play yard.

Juke Joints

Juke joints were places in the colored community to socialize with friends. Food and drinks were sold. A jukebox is a partially automated music machine that operates when coins are inserted. There was a bench that ran about halfway around the room, a jukebox, a dance floor, and a service counter. Mr. Henry's family lived in the back. My sisters were allowed to go and dance and have fun. Curfew for them was ten o'clock. I was not old enough to go at all, unless it was during daylight hours to make a purchase, as dictated by Mama.

There was another colored-owned business in the neighborhood called Mr. Perry's Place. Mr. Perry had a smaller place and his family lived upstairs. The same kind of activities took place there as at Mr. Henry's joint. We always wondered, though, how Mr. Perry could swing around on his crutches, collecting the items we wanted and how he managed to get upstairs with his crutches. He sold the same items as Mr. Henry but included hot sandwiches and cigarettes. A favorite item was the large sugar cookies. He also sold bootleg liquor because ours was a dry county; this meant that it was illegal to sell or buy liquor. Everybody knew where to get liquor, but it had to be handled very discreetly, especially around kids.

<u>Churches</u>

We had our own churches in our own neighborhood, including two Baptist churches, a Methodist Church, and a Church of God in Christ. People tended to eat after church services on Sundays. This was particularly true in the southern states. However, it has not always been that way. Colored or Negro-owned eating establishments were few in the days when I grew up. Black communities in the south were not permitted to eat in restaurants with white patrons. Pastors were often not residents of our town but came in on Sundays for church services.

Since going out to eat was not an option, a Sunday tradition emerged in the Black churches that seemed to work. A family signed up for the Sunday they would volunteer to feed Pastor and his family in the interim between morning, Baptist Training Union (BTU) and evening services. The volunteer family invited Pastor to their homes to eat and relax before evening services began. It has been said, and I have heard it said, that this practice caused problems in many marriages. The meal might have consisted of a beef roast or fried chicken, along with the hostess's best side items and a favorite dessert.

Mama brought the preacher home many times. Pastor got preferential treatment on that day. He was served first and got the best piece of the chicken. I was a child looking on. It did seem like Daddy was unhappy with the arrangement because he refused to partake of that meal. Children got to eat when all the grown-ups were finished. The children did the clean-up while adults talked with Pastor and his family, until time for the next service.

<u>Meet Racism</u>

Most of the things we needed could be gotten in the neighborhood. Mr. Dyers' store was a white family-owned grocery store and one pump gas station, at the fork in the road where the outskirts of the Colored community intertwined with the white community. We could walk to the store to get things that Mama needed, like a loaf of bread or a few eggs. Going out of the neighborhood did not happen often. Outside the neighborhood, there was a different world. Our little town was a part of that world, so much so that going to town was special because it gave us something different to do.

By the early 1960s I found out that white citizens in our little town made the rules. Many times, the rules or laws were made up on the spot. These were Jim Crow laws, made up and applicable only to Colored citizens. I did not know that before because I lived in a Colored world. The 'Whites Only' signs were so obvious in town and so was the practice of keeping my eyes and head focused away and cast downward if I met a white person on the street. There were two unspoken rules: do not make waves, and do not do anything that could be misconstrued as breaking a rule. I do not ever remember having a conversation about segregation or civil rights or how to react to white people on their turf.

Interracial dating was also strongly prohibited. This act alone could cause alienation with the whites, possible abuse and becoming an outcast in town. One of our neighbors grew up and moved to Chicago. When he came back to Cadiz, he brought his wife, a white woman, with him. I heard whispers, as a child, that he was harassed and threatened. It was not long before he moved away again.

My siblings and I played and joked as we walked along, going to town. The town was a rural area but there were sidewalks. I had to be careful to walk along the grassy right of way. I only went to town with an older sibling, because of the danger lurking there. Sometimes white boys or men in cars would drive right up next to us, as we walked on the grass and they would swerve quickly into our path as we walked, causing us to jump out of the way. We sometimes jumped into a ditch nearby or down a steep incline to avoid being hit by the oncoming vehicle. It was not safe to be on that stretch of road leading to town where there were no sidewalks.

Once I got to the two-block shopping area, there were concrete sidewalks. When I turned the corner, I could see Fred's Florist Shop just beyond a flashing yellow light, cautioning and welcoming me; the candy-striped pole of Frank's Barber Shop, with its 'Whites Only' sign, Gus's Western Auto Store, with its brightly painted bicycles, tricycles with training wheels and horns attached, shiny yellow dump trucks, and white dolls with long blonde hair and pretty dresses. Cadiz Café downtown had arrows directing 'Coloreds' to a back or side door for service. For service, I was taught to go to that designated back door and knock on it for service. There might be a long wait before we were served. There was also a water fountain standing near the county courthouse, with its 'Coloreds Only' sign. There was a clothing store where Mama had a line of credit. Five and Dime Store was a favorite for us. We might have a nickel to spend on 'penny candy' like lollipops and bubble gum. It was priced so we might get three pieces of our choice of candy for a penny.

Trigg County Farmer's Bank and Hardware Store made up the other shopping stores on Main Street. At the far end of town, stood a lumber and construction establishment. The post office sat on this same street, high up on a hill.

The local drug store had a counter where white children could sit and have ice cream sodas and other delights. I stood outside the plate glass door and decorated windows, watching wistfully, mesmerized, as those children of the privileged in our town, sat giggling and talking and enjoying their ice cream treats. I did not go to town often, but I wished that I could have that moment for my friends and me.

Daddy bought block ice by the pound to put in the icebox in our kitchen for keeping food cool. As a special treat, occasionally, Mama made homemade ice cream in an old-fashioned hand-crank ice cream maker. It was a wonderful treat for us, but it did not erase the longing that I had to be sharing a treat with friends in a public place.

Most of our dry goods were purchased in Hopkinsville, where there were more stores and more variety. Daddy would take us there once a year to get new shoes and household items. This trip eliminated the need for going to town except to collect our mail. Before the age of twelve, I was not allowed to go to town without adult supervision.

Years later, I read about the treatment of Blacks in the South, in the days when when we were 'Colored'. After we were 'Colored', the terminology was 'Negro'. I did not know what was meant by Jim Crow laws, as such, and of course they were not openly called that, but the adults knew that it meant that 'Colored' people practiced staying in line, staying in their place. That is what they taught their children. I was practicing obeying unwritten laws without knowing it. We had no place, other than that of servitude. When walking on the sidewalk, for instance, if I encountered a white person, I would have to my keep eyes down, focused on some invisible object on the ground. Then I would step off the sidewalk and stay there until the white person passed.

Walking with my parents or older siblings, I would feel a hand pressed on my shoulder, and in a quiet voice, would say, "Move over," as they gently guided me to do that. My parents practiced this, but they did not talk about it.

Town was the place where we met up with racism and abuse. Discrimination was all around us. By the time I was thirteen, I, with Ollie or Grady, or alone walked to town to retrieve the mail from our post office box. I could go alone. One day, on my way there as I walked alone, I turned the corner by the stop sign and I saw a white man in a clean, late modeled, car. He had stopped at the same stop sign, as he was supposed to. However, he stayed stopped a moment too long. That got my attention and when I glanced over into the car, I could see that he was wearing a white shirt and necktie but no pants or underwear. Horrified, I ran for the post office because I knew there would be people there. I constantly looked behind me when I left the post office to go home. I was afraid. I got home safely and without incident. From then on, I was cautious when I went out of the neighborhood.

I never told my parents about that or that time the husband of the woman Mama worked for at the restaurant's hotel, cleaning toilets and making beds, and cleaning the restaurant from the night before activities. One Saturday morning, as I worked, he had asked me to bring soda pop drinks for he and his three friends, as they sat around a table.

When I brought the drinks, he grabbed my behind, saying, "Come here, girl!"

As I pushed away and ran to find Mama, who was in another room, I could hear them clapping and laughing as I fled. Mistreatment and abuse were commonplace. There was no point in filing a claim or anything; it was best just to let it go. That is what I was taught. Do not make waves. I learned to overlook or put up with things that I suspected were wrong.

<u>Separate, but Equal?</u>

Aunt Marie sponsored the Drama/Speech Club, which I participated in during middle school. Carol, Dot, Eve, and I learned to enunciate, memorize, make eye contact with the judges, proper elocution, and correct posture in front of judges. I loved learning the works of poetry and prose written by Black composers and others. We put in a lot of hours of practice, after school. Aunt Marie was archaic but prodded the best out of her speech team. We participated at competitions around local and district churches. I don't remember any of my speeches.

Truthfully, I don't think I was ever proficient. However, it served me well when I became a teacher and was in front of groups of people every day. I was able to see its benefits. I was always comfortable in that role.

As a youngster, I had been a happy, carefree child, participating in our segregated separate but equal community activities. Things weren't equal, but it was what we had.

How could I feel equal when at every chance some called me a derogatory name or made insinuating gestures at me? Had we not used secondhand books for years in our segregated schools? Church activities were fun, singing in the choir, leading the songs, singing solo parts, and aspiring to be another Aretha Franklin or Mahalia Jackson. Here, things were equal; nothing could be taken away.

4-H Clubs were sponsored by the State Department of Agriculture. The four H's stood for Head, Heart, Hands, and Health. We learned to use each of the body parts to help us have a more productive life. Again, this club was separate but not equal. We had the opportunity to participate in activities but in a different, and less colorful environment. For instance, our activities were held in someone's home. Competitions were held in neighborhood churches. Our white counterparts had use of community buildings. It was all segregated, but we had the opportunity to do things that we otherwise would not have done in our community.

Our white advisors worked for and were paid by the state of Kentucky, provided forms and information to our leaders who arranged competition meetings, field trips, and competitions between the adjoining county. The top 4-H Club winners of blue ribbon at the county level were rewarded with a trip to the state convention or 4-H Club camp. I always had entries in several categories to make sure of my summer trip. To practice, I baked dozens of cookies, biscuits, and cornbread. I sewed aprons, skirts, and blouses.

My family had a sewing machine, and my older sisters could sew, so they were able to help our leader to ensure everything was made. Our leader was Mrs. Bertha, but we called her, "Miss Noonie". I participated in the public speaking category, as well.

At fourteen years old, I earned the opportunity to go to a trip to the state capital. Once in Frankfort, away from parents and family, we saw a different perspective. Kentucky State University was a historically Black university, in the lovely town of Frankfort, where the government of Kentucky operates. We saw that Colored-Negro people could do well in a white-dominated world. We learned that we could be educated and be whatever we wanted to be.

We went to the usual sightseeing trips to the capital, businesses, the state penitentiary, the floral clock, the history center, old state house buildings, and beautiful architecture. We were assigned rooms in one of the dorms. Meals were prepared for us for the entire week. We were given a travel go bag for lunch on the road.

Even then, white people would harass us, by asking questions like, "Where'd you get the money to pay for this?" Sometimes, they would yell, "Go eat in your neighborhood!" Bathroom breaks were a different story. We had to plan ahead to find where we could stop and eat. The bus driver and chaperones knew which towns had 'Colored Only' public restrooms. We waited until we found one where we were welcomed.

Even through segregation, it was still a grand old time. We made friends from other counties. I had the opportunity to bathe in showers without worrying if the hot water would run out, use indoor toilets, and sleep in rooms with locks on the doors. We did not have those at home. Our chaperones were awesome, too. They let us enjoy ourselves, pranks, and all. I had the chance to experience this trip at least two times. Traveling on back roads, on an old un-air-conditioned bus in the early 1960's, making stops, picking up students in Trigg, Christian, and Todd Counties was quite the trip. It was the ultimate experience because most of us had never been anywhere outside our neighborhoods.

While we were at the state convention, one of the activities called for dressing up. I brought the outfit Mama packed for me to wear. My girlfriend, Carol, had a real cute little pink and white gingham dress, with capped sleeves, princess neckline, and a yellow bow, that she had brought as an extra. She and I were about the same size, so she said that I could wear her extra dress.

When she saw me admiring, "Wear it", Carol insisted. I was proud of the way I looked in that dress. Twirling around like a model, I wore Carol's dress to the awards ceremony in the afternoon. I took the dress home to wash and return later.

When I got home, Mama was practically yelling as she was helping me unpack, "What is this? Ann, this ain't yours! Whose is it?" Then, in a soft voice, she admonished, "You will wear what we can afford for you to wear. Alright, now, let's get this dress washed and ironed and back to Carol."

The lesson I learned from that experience was that Mama said I would wear what I could afford, and I should not borrow from other people just to make myself look better or feel better. I carried this lesson with me even through college, while I lived in the dorm with other like-minded, same-sized girls. I never did borrow or trade clothes. I had what I could afford to buy, and I wore what I had.

My father owned a car, purchased his home site in 1949, owned his own tractor, and for a while, a cow, and some pigs. He farmed his property raising tobacco, corn, and a full garden of fruits and vegetables. There were several fruit trees on our property, so we had an abundance of apples, peaches, grapes, pears, and persimmons. There was also a walnut tree. According to the standards of the 1950s and 1960s, we were well off in the neighborhood. With ten children, there were plenty of hands and feet to do the work.

Daddy was also a sharecropper. Tobacco was taken to market just before Christmas, usually, and we always got something new for Christmas. I usually got a pair of black and white Oxford shoes and a toy, white plastic doll, candy, and oranges. My brothers got a pull toy like a wagon or tricycle, and the candy and oranges.

So, this trip was important. Did we stay home and not go anywhere to keep us safe in the world of hatred and bigotry? Was it to provide a sense of well-being and community value? I do not remember ever being faced with protesters or police yelling for our rights. But in 1963, with state-mandated integration, I found the hatred for us to be ingrained in the white students' way of life and behavior.

Chapter 4

CHANGING TIMES

City Water

We had just gotten running water inside our house in late 1959. Water lines had been put through our neighborhood to accommodate the building of a new school close by. There were pipes and a single spigot put in through the kitchen floor. This made a major difference in our household. No more trips out back to draw water from the cistern.

Things were better at home because Daddy had the neighborhood carpenter add a bathroom onto the back of our house. It had the necessary equipment: toilet, tub, washbasin, an accordion sliding door made of corrugated vinyl. This meant that there was very little privacy when you were in the bathroom. Entry to the bathroom was directly from Mama and Daddy's bedroom, but we were so glad to have it.

This was part of the step up my parents had anticipated when they made the move from Ditney Ridge. We no longer had to use an outhouse or bring in an old metal tub and fill it with water to take a bath. Home life and school life were changing. Daddy added to the house again a few years later by putting a large bedroom, with closets, on the back of the house, beyond the kitchen.

In the mid-60s, Ollie and I used our money we saved from afterschool jobs to buy Mama an electric washer. This made it easier for her to complete the laundry. Since it was an easier process, we could do the laundry and hang it on the clotheslines to dry. No more heating water and struggling with the old crank washer. The new washer was placed in the bathroom, to make use of the plumbing already in place.

A School Just for Us

In 1959, the state built the Colored-Negro children a new school in the neighborhood, called McUpton School. That was segregation in full force, but it was not new. We had been segregated at Dunbar, as well. Dunbar was closed. It sat up on that hill many years, desolate. except for the memories and secrets it kept. I went to McUpton school in its opening year when I was in third through eighth grade. I do not recall anybody ever explaining how it came to be named. Mr. Edward Oats was our first principal. Then in 1963, laws were passed outlawing segregation, aiming for racial equality.

McUpton was a brand-new school for Negro children in the County. This was the first county in the state to completely integrate its schools. It was said by some that it may have been an attempt to avoid desegregation. The older people in the community liked that we had a school in our community just for their children. They felt proud that children were going to school. It worked.

The white community was satisfied that their white children would not be subjected to Colored children in the schools. The Negro community not only had a school, but it gained much more. It meant having a community building where meetings could be held, large groups of food could be served, like family reunions, a place for playing basketball and a place that employed Negro workers. The building would be maintained by the county. Children got a hot lunch in the cafeteria for $0.20 to $0.25 per day. A long-held dream had come true. Then, disaster struck. The white high school was destroyed by fire in 1960. At the same time, the Christian

County Schools system determined that Attucks High school could no longer accept Colored high school students from Trigg County because of over-crowding in their own district. Other arrangements had to be made.

Trigg County School Board decided to fill McUpton with as many students as possible from Negro and white communities. The numbers of third and fourth graders in both Negro and white schools from the whole county would fill the school. McUpton then became a school for all students in grades three and four in 1966. All other students attended school on the main campus of Trigg County Schools.

Several portables were used to house middle school students in the beginning. Construction began shortly afterward, to replace the portables. When the new addition was completed, all students were moved to the main campus.

High School

The day had come but nothing in my world had prepared me for that opening day of school in August 1963. This was the guinea pig class. We were the students who were integrating the county school system for the first time. Colored and white students were thrown in together and it would be sink or swim. I did not fully understand the real impact until I walked into a classroom on that first day at the newly built space filled with predominately white faces, mostly white teachers, students, principals, and cafeteria workers. We were stared at and greeted with tentative smiles and wide-eyed fear. The white students were afraid, as we were, but they showed kindness and tried to be helpful. It was a new experience for everyone. In retrospect, they took away my identity that day. I would have to work hard to get it back.

I did not understand why I had to be there. It required me to change.

The new Trigg County High School was built in a prominent white neighborhood of Cadiz. Some white citizens complained about Negro children using the sidewalks around their homes when going to and from school buildings. The Superintendent solved that problem by having a school bus pick the Negro children up to take them to and from school, even though they lived within walking distance of the school. All this was to get us out the white community. The Negro students met at specified bus stops in the Negro community.

I witnessed some altercations at the high school and some name calling that led to fights. It was a regular occurrence to be called "nigger". For the most part, the transition happened smoothly. Some of the teachers showed attitudes that indicated they would rather not be teaching us. Others seemed to take it as a privilege. We seemed to be doing well in the schools with integration, but other parts of the country were struggling. States like Georgia and Mississippi and Alabama were resisting the call for integrating. The Civil Rights movement took on a life of its own, headed by non-violent advocates like Dr. Martin Luther King, Jr.

Surprisingly, it did not seem to affect my family's world. We just kept doing what we had always done—we did not make waves.

The students who came in as seniors in 1963 were the first Negro students to graduate from the newly integrated school. In 1966, a Negro girl was chosen to be on the Basketball Queen's Court. Her name was Dot.

In 1967, chosen from the first Negro class to graduate from the integrated school, having completed grades 9-12, students and faculty chose a Negro as Basketball Queen. Her name was Carol. It was said the smooth transition of integration was in part because Negro boys were a major part of the sports program. They made winning teams in football, basketball and track and field events. This smoothed the feathers of those in the white community who did not want integration, according to the Superintendent at the time.

I learned to be a part of the high school scene. I made the honor roll consistently, so I was invited to join the Beta Club, the equivalent of todays' National Honor Society. Several of my friends and I joined the Pep Club, making signs and hanging them around the school. We boarded buses to travel to the away games to support our interracial teams. I wanted to be a writer, so I joined the Journalism Club and the school newspaper. I enrolled in business classes to learn to type. I wanted to get along with whites and blacks. But I sensed that most of the white students did not like me, as they smiled at me.

When I saw these same students in town, they did not smile, but rather turned their head away. The 'Whites Only' signs in town were immediately taken down, along with the signs urging Coloreds to go to the back door for takeout service at restaurants. The thing about that was everybody still remembered where they had been and what they had stood for. Sports were for boys during my high school years. It changed soon after I graduated, but there was still not a girls' basketball team. I was tall and agile enough that I was sure I could have played. Adjacent counties had girls' teams in their programs. Our school had track and field events, but not for girls. We were not even allowed to wear shorts unless we had a skirt over it. Aunt Marie, who taught at the school (the only female Negro teacher there) was especially adamant about us not showing our knees.

It was a time when girls wore dresses and skirts at knee length or longer. Pants were not permitted. Many of my clothes were passed down from Mama's white workhouses. I wore poodle skirts, gathered skirts with a waistband, blouses that buttoned down the front or with Peter Pan collars, penny loafers and bobby socks. My hair was hot-combed so it would hand straight or be curled. I was fitting into my new school environment.

Change was to be found in our new nomenclature. It was during this time that black power with Malcolm X was pushing politics, opposing Dr. Martin Luther King in his nonviolence advocacy. We had gone from being Colored to Negro to being Black. This is the name that was chosen for us by our own, touting black power as the way. The violent and volatile activities so prevalent in the more southern states with a higher percentage of Black citizens, who were largely uneducated, illiterate, and non-voting did not affect or reach my little part of the world in Cadiz, Kentucky. Political rallies and protest marches, sit-ins, shouting matches, and organized protests were met with increased numbers of lynches and disappearances of people trying to make things better. I had never heard of Ku Klux Klan activities in our county, though they probably existed. I stayed in my neighborhood and did not make waves. I was happy there.

Falling in love for the first time happened in high school, during this time of mayhem and change. I was finally able to go to the Juke joint at Mr. Henry's and have some fun. Mama allowed me to go, but I had to ask permission each time, so she knew where I was. I danced to the juke box to the popular hits of Jackie Wilson, The Miracles, The Four Tops and James Brown. I swayed to the slow tunes of Chubby Checker and Etta James. Girls sat on the benches along the walls or stood around and waited for the boys to ask us to dance. Lew, another one of my friends, confessed his love for me, many times. I was still in school but he had dropped out of school. Lew wanted to marry me. He drove a fast car, a '57 Chevy, that he kept revved up. His car made a deafening roar as he raced up and down the road in front of my house.

Mama, sitting on the front porch having her Pepsi, observed, "That boy is too wild. One day, he is gonna hurt himself. And maybe somebody else, too. Stay away from him."

"But Mama, he loves me", I'd say, pretending to be hurt.

"Stay away from him," Mama repeated, sternly.

And of course, every time I got a chance I'd go for a ride with him or let him walk me home. She continued to warn me away from Lew, but when you are a teenager, danger looks enticing.

Mama was right. Lew did have two really devastating car accidents. The last one damaged his spine and left him without the use of his legs. After surgery and recuperation, he went back to driving, but more sensibly, in his car that was specially equipped to be operated using hand controls.

It was common to be told to go back to "nigger-town" if we were out of our neighborhood, but white citizens were commonly seen in our area, whether to pick up their Colored housekeepers, to drop off or pick up their laundry, or even just to antagonize us. Laundry day meant that my family, the girls especially, used an old-fashioned iron that was heated by setting it on the flat, hot top of a wood or coal burning stove to iron clothes all day. Dress shirts were previously starched with a mixture of cornstarch and cold water. Each shirt had to be sprinkled with water, prior to ironing, to get rid of the creases and wrinkles. Mama inspected each piece that we ironed. Some pieces had to be re-ironed.

This increased the family's income by two to three dollars per week. Occasionally, the employer would bring fresh fish that he caught on his last fishing trip. That was a real treat for us! Most of the families that Mama worked for had children close to our ages, so we were gifted with outgrown hand-me-downs for my sister and me. At the same time, I refused to wear their hand-me-downs because I did not want to be teased about it. I had no way of knowing who had worn what.

I sewed most of my clothes and bought others using money from my after-school jobs of babysitting and working at the nursing home. I had to deal with white people in our town in different ways, depending on what the situation was. At school it was time for warm and friendly. When they were not in school, we became "niggers" again, being looked past, as if invisible.

Upheaval

Even though I did not like high school, I did like my neighborhood. I felt comfortable there. On weekends, sometimes Daddy barbecued a whole sheep or goat meat on his self-made barbeque pit/grill in the backyard. My brothers rigged a bright light in the yard. It always turned into an all-night fun affair. Daddy sat outside all night, manning the grill. Neighbors brought beer and cold pop. When the meat was tender and browned, the sun was usually coming up, then Daddy mopped the meat one final time with his special homemade barbecue sauce, banked the wood under the grill and went inside to go to bed. Buster took over the work of serving. Mama made some potato salad and coleslaw to go with the meat. People dropped by, visiting, and waiting to get a sandwich. Daddy's coveted barbecue sauce and burgoo were big hits. Everybody wanted the recipe. These were the special times that I cherish in my memories of Daddy.

There were times when Daddy was mean, too. One day, I heard him yelling and cussing at one of the men he carpooled with. He looked up and saw that I overheard him and threatened to whip me. He did whip me on occasion, but it was usually Mama who handled discipline. So, the family was surprised when Daddy, out of the blue, committed a heinous act of violence.

"Cock-a-doodle-do!" Our lone rooster crowed at the break of day just as every other day. Daddy got up early, per usual, to prepare for the day's activities. This day, he did not prepare for work. Instead, our father had walked out of the house that morning, before any of us had gotten ready for school, taking his shotgun with him. He did not speak to anyone. Nor did he tell anyone what was about to happen. Daddy walked over to Aunt Marie's yard, onto the farthest corner.

There, her husband, his brother-in-law, was digging a ditch. Daddy did not speak to him. He raised his loaded weapon. And shot him. Chaos erupted. Neighbors came running out of their houses to see what the noise was. Daddy was calm, but he still spoke to no one. He walked back into our house, put the gun away, picked up the telephone and called the police.

"I just shot a man. Come on out here and pick me up."

After listening for a minute, he said, "Yes, I will be waiting for you."

This happened in 1964. The white police came.

"What have you done?... Come on, we will take you downtown," he said. The police took him away. Meanwhile, someone called for an ambulance, as Uncle lay bleeding on the hardened dirt.

We got word a little later that Uncle would be alright. He was not seriously hurt. Daddy had used his shotgun, which does less harm. We were at a loss that early morning about what to do. It would take years for me to understand the full impact of what Daddy had done. With that one single act, our family was torn apart. His brothers and sisters chose sides. Yes, it was like the typical feuds characterized in the Appalachian Mountains area. There was no more gunfire, but two of Daddy's sisters did not speak a word to him, nor he to them, for about twenty-five years.

Whenever his brothers visited town, they came over to our house to visit. Aunt Marie's children were no longer our daily playmates and best friend cousins. Our family had to face the gruesome and unsettling fact that there was an invisible line drawn, separating the two families and two properties—ours and theirs.

When the judge sentenced Daddy to be incarcerated for the unfortunate deed that he had done, the whole family was upset and had their own different ways of dealing with it. He admitted that he had done the deed, accepted his punishment and served his time in the county jail.

He was released from jail and remanded to the State Mental Institution for treatment of paranoid schizophrenia. When the treatment was finished, Daddy came home. There was palatable stigma associated with his having a mental disease. The rest of the family had a difficult time trying to figure out how to react to him when he was released. It was hard to know how to accept him. He was different. The neighborhood knew about the incident and some of them probably were witnesses to it, but nobody made fun of us. I think the neighbors sympathized with us and wanted to help us deal with the situation, but they stayed out of Daddy's way.

Daddy always kept a shotgun in his bedroom above the door leading to the kitchen. We knew that it was handy and loaded. He also kept a pistol under his pillow at night. I did not know where he kept that pistol in the daytime. But, I wondered. It was probably in his pocket. I tried to stay away from him as much as possible. As a youngster, I heard many fights and arguments. I did not know what the fights with Mama were about. It was as if suddenly Daddy was out of control and anything could set him off. Another person or personality took over his body, it seemed.

Daddy called Mama some awful words…

"B*tch." He threatened her with his pistol, waving it, saying, "I will shoot you, you high yellow b*tch."

"Go on then, shoot me", she'd holler back at him. Just as quickly, Daddy became docile, mumbling to himself, went back to his chair or to bed.

Relieved, I found my way out of the hostile area. I went out to play or to bed, pulling covers over my head. I prayed that Daddy would love Mama and not hurt her. He never did shoot her, though, or at her. Daily routine had been tough at home when my father left, but when he returned, life became more strange. It was getting closer to time for me to move on to further my education. Mama insisted on my going to college. I was ready to leave the house of poverty and abuse.

Chapter 5

HIGHER EDUCATION

School and Work

Graduation from Trigg County High School as a member of that first class having integrated the system was a milestone. We were celebrated. Several of the Colored students had dropped out along the way so we were proud to represent all of us. After high school, I was accepted at Hopkinsville Community College (University of Kentucky), Murray State College, and Western Kentucky University colleges. It made me feel proud to know that I was good enough to get into those schools. I received a scholarship from Trigg County Farmers Bank to cover my tuition for the Community College in Hopkinsville, Kentucky.

Immediately after graduating high school, Carol and I took a trip to Indianapolis. She stayed for one week and then went on to her summer job. I stayed on with my brother, Nat. I spent the summer in Indianapolis, living at his house. While I lived with him, I got a job as a cashier at a nearby grocery store. It was only a few blocks from his house so I could walk to work. I was a part-time cashier, so I had time to do fun things in the city. Nat went to his construction job religiously, seldom missing any days. He worked hard.

On weekends he drank lots of alcohol. One weekend he drank some liquor, and then he drank some more, until he became very angry. I had seen his temper on previous weekends when he had hit his wife. One night, as his wife sat watching, he started to hit me with his fists, after he declared vehemently that he did not want fish for dinner.

"Stop! Stop! You're hurting me!" I shouted at him. He did not stop but continued to swear at me as I ran around tables and chairs.

"Help me," I begged my sister-in-law.

She just shook her head "no", and I knew why. As I ran through the kitchen and past the skillet of hot grease on the stove, Nat was directly behind me, I reached for the handle of the skillet, but he saw my intention, grabbed the skillet, and moved it out of my reach. I was surprised he did not throw the grease on me. He was just that angry.

That evening, he pummeled me with his construction man's fists until I was too weak to run anymore. I was too young to know that abuse is never right, and the abusers do not stop. I thought family members should care more about each other. I did know that I needed to get away from Nat and to a place of safety, so I called my brother, Buster, to come and pick me up. He came right away after I explained what had happened. He and his friends doctored my two black eyes and pampered me for a couple of days. Although Nat apologized for his behavior later, our relationship was splintered, and I had a hard time being in the same room with him.

When it was time for me to go to college, I asked Daddy to complete my financial aid forms. It took a long time for him to sign the papers. I assumed it was because he did not want to send another of his girls to school. Eventually, he signed them, with Mama's encouragement. I got the things I needed to go to Hopkinsville Community College, except a car. I arranged to get a ride with one of the white girls, Kae, from my high school class, who had been in many of my classes over the course of four years at Trigg County High. She and her sister drove over to my neighborhood to pick me up on the days when we all had classes at the same times.

Other days, Buster drove me two other Negro classmates' house and I rode with them. I attended the Community College for three semesters. After the first year, I bought a used Ford Falcon from my summer job savings. I had worked with my sister, Jean, at Elk Brand Manufacturing Company. I sat on that boring assembly line making clothing out of seemingly endless bolts of blue denim fabric. In the fall of 1968, the sock factory, Trigg Knit, hired me full-time.

One job nightmare was traded for another. I was responsible for ten fully loaded machines that ran continuously to make the factory-mandated production. Working the graveyard shift, I went to school in the mornings, did homework and slept in the afternoon. By eleven o'clock in the evening, I was back at the factory. My shift ended at seven o'clock in the mornings, Sunday through Thursday. Then, I went home to get ready for school. I repeated the whole activity schedule. Mama said there is always a lesson for me in hard times, but sometimes I had to look closely to find that lesson. I needed to finish my education because I could not envision myself doing factory assembly line work a minute longer than I had to. I was neither coordinated or fast enough to keep all those machines running and emptied of socks. Two other Black women worked that shift. They often helped me out by coming over and pulling and snipping socks from my machines.

It was finally time, in 1968, for me to leave my father's house. Daddy and I did not see eye-to-eye on many things. And I longed for the chance to move away for years. I loved my father because he was Daddy, but our relationship had deteriorated to the point that I could not see mending it. It was tough to be in the house with Daddy. He would hum to himself in a most annoying way. When friends came over,

I was uncomfortable. I did not know what he might do. He was not mean or violent at this time, but I felt like I was walking on eggshells, tiptoeing around, waiting for something to explode.

When I came home from school, I tried talking to Daddy but could not have a conversation beyond speaking a pleasant "hello". One of the things that puzzled me for a long time was that he thought I had put something in his shoes that would hurt him. He also thought I was trying to poison him.

He started making his own food and kept close watch over everything that went on in the house. I know it was the mental disease causing him to display modified behavior, but it still hurt that we could not communicate. Daddy insisted *I* was trying to cause harm to him. I could tell by the way he acted when I was in the house that he did not trust me. Mama encouraged me to stay out of his way. Other arrangements were made so I could finish school.

Mama's Aunt Essie lived in Hopkinsville. She allowed me to live her in her spare room. I moved in with Aunt Essie and started working at the Christian County Department of Agriculture Office, assisting with 4-H clubs in the county. I continued to take classes at the local college. This lasted until I had finished my third semester at the Community College. I changed my major and pursued something else.

I realized I needed a plan, so I made one. I took the hours that I had earned at the Community College in transfer to Western Kentucky University, which was about a two-hour drive away. I moved into the dormitory and this was where I lived until the middle of my junior year. At the Community College I had planned to transfer to University of Kentucky to earn a degree in English Journalism.

The problem was they did not offer that degree at Western Kentucky University and that's where my scholarship was. I made the decision to switch to Western and majored in Home Economics Education. I moved into the dormitory there and discovered a whole new world. Sharing a room was nothing new to me since that was part of my family life from the beginning, usually with three other people instead of two. And I did have my own twin-size bed, desk, and closet. I loved Western. I was part of the work study program on campus and worked about twenty-five hours each week for minimum wage of $1.60 per hour. That provided me with necessities and spending money. But I gained something more valuable; I had freedom to do as I pleased. I did not go home very often, except for the major holidays, because the dorms were closed.

My habit of keeping a diary compelled me to write all my most intimate thoughts. I found the love of my life at age nineteen. Ron will tell you that he saw me on the steps at Mr. Henry's wearing a miniskirt and a long polka dot tie.

"I'm going to marry that girl," he said more than once. He was a year behind me in high school, but we became friends, and I finally decided to go out with him. He had a swagger and a mesmerizing smile. Ron and I did many things together. I was comfortable in the neighborhood, more so than at school. Even though I was a part of clubs and activities, I always felt I was not accepted in the integrated activities, like I should not be there. Maybe it was how I had always been treated that caused me to feel this way.

By this time, I had known Ron for more than two years and we were good friends. I thought I wanted to have a life with him. He had a kind and generous attitude and made me smile and laugh. I think what I liked most was that Ron was pleasant and polite to everyone.

When we were at Mr. Henry's Place, he would ask, "You wanna dance with me?"

Giggling, I would step into his arms, smiling widely. We would dance a slow two-step with our bodies pressed tight together, moving slowly to a Marvin Gaye or Aretha Franklin song about love. To be young and in love feels like the whole universe is aligned just for you and that there is perfection at the end.

Ron and I spent as much time together as we could. He was living and working in Indianapolis. Giving myself a vacation from school, one weekend, I rode the Greyhound bus to visit him, a few months after I had moved into the dorm at Western. Mama had not given me permission to leave school for that little trip. I prayed that she would not find out about it. She did not think Ron was the right guy for me. But, Ron and I shared similar goals and aspirations. Both of us wanted something more than was available in Cadiz.

Our backgrounds were alike in that our families were economically low income. His, because his single mother was raising four sons. Ron was the oldest. He loved playing cards and gambling. Having no idea what he wanted to do with his life, he just decided to try the military as his way out of our town and poverty. He joined the Army in October of 1970 and immediately began his basic training. I was pregnant when he left. Mama was not pleased. That was not what she wanted for me in that season of my life.

I withdrew the second semester of my junior year of college. I needed a job to pay for the expense of giving birth and providing for a baby and myself, not yet sure of the role Ron would take in the baby's life. Ron had not figured out the military at that time. I got a job working during the summer at the Lake Barkley State Park Resort, near Cadiz. My job was working in the kitchen. I worked full-time and saved my money. I made payments to the doctor monthly to cover the birth of my baby. When summer jobs ended, my friend Carol asked me to move in with her at Murray State University in Murray, Kentucky. She needed someone to be the nanny for her toddler while she attended classes and worked. She was separated from her husband at that time. I agreed because Mama was still upset with me because I had gotten pregnant and had to leave school. And I was very uncomfortable being in the house with Daddy and her all day, every day.

I moved to Murray. Val, Carol's toddler, was a happy little girl. It was easy to care for her. I was glad to help Carol out. I stayed there with them in her trailer with the leaky roof and drafty windows until the end of November. It was the time of year for tornadoes. I managed through one major tornado and although the trailer rocked on its platform, it did not turn over or lose its roof. But it was very scary.

Shortly after the storm, I went home to wait for the birth of my baby. While Ron was getting his basic training, stationed in Georgia, our son was born. My sister, Jean, was there for me, offering kindness, as usual. She drove me to the hospital when I went into labor, and stayed with me until my baby was born. I named him Nick. Ron got a leave from the Army and came home a few days later. I had missed him horribly and wished he could have been at the hospital with me. Then, I wished I could go with him when he left. That was not to be.

Mama insisted that I go back to school in January. It was the first semester of my senior year. I wanted to wait until my baby was older. Nick was only four weeks old. Mama convinced me to leave Nick with her until I finished school. It was hard to do. First, Ron was gone and then I left my baby. It felt like part of me was missing. My heart hurt terribly. Nevertheless, I moved back into the dorm at Western.

I lived in the dorm one semester. This time, I had to get a student loan because I had dropped out and my scholarship had lapsed. My old friends were still there but they would graduate in the spring. For the entire year of 1971, I concentrated on getting my degree. I went home as much as possible to spend time with my infant son. I did make a few new friends, but I did not have time for friends or a social life.

For the next two sessions, I rented an apartment in Bowling Green, Kentucky. I stayed there for seven months in my little apartment. It was freedom. I loved being on my own. My son stayed with me part of the time, but I had a job and classes, so he also stayed with Mama or Aunt Cora. After I graduated, I moved back home with my parents. I was dissatisfied there. I knew I needed to be in my own place. I knew I needed to be making my own way.

Chapter 6

A DIFFERENT LIFE

<u>Moves and Marriage Proposal</u>

Ron's first assignment after basic training was to Korea. He was going overseas. It would be a thirteen-month assignment.

One evening when we were together, he said to me, "You wanna get married?"

I just looked at him as if to say, "What kind of proposal is that?"

"Let me put it this way: do you want to marry me?"

I still had not answered.

So, he asked again, nervously, "Will you marry me?"

I could tell that he was nervous because he kept rubbing the back of his neck. I was enjoying his discomfort, so I looked at him and grinned, happily, "Yes! Yes! Let's do it! I want to marry you!" We hugged and then he kissed me.

"We will be a family. Anything you want, you only need to tell me," he urged.

"I'm not sure how all this works, but I love Nick and you. We can figure it out together."

We talked about being married and having more children and the impact that his being in the Army would have on all of us. I did not realize that day the extent of our commitment to each other.

One evening, we decided on a date that was prior to his going overseas. I gave Ron my heart and we embarked on an incredible journey that taught me how wonderful life could be even through all its twists, turns, ups and downs, heartaches, heart breaks, as well as the delightful things that happen along the way. I learned to savor it all as we grew up together. Sometimes, he was working, and other times, he was out playing cards with friends, or being a family man. He loved playing cards in those early days in the military.

Ron sometimes displayed a unique sense of humor, adventuresome and fun-loving. He could tell you a joke or story and you would find yourself chuckling days later. I knew that he loved me, as I loved him. I loved his Army stories, as well. As a young soldier, he was trying to decide whether he wanted to be an airborne certified soldier. Plus, time was ripe for a new experience.

He said, "I'm going to parachute out of an airplane to see if I like it."

Puzzled, I asked, "Why would you do that?"

"Because I am scared to do it."

"That makes a lot of sense… to somebody."

"No, it does make sense." He tried to convince me.

"I am scared to do it but I want to do it to prove to myself that I can. I have taken the class and I know what to do. To get certified as an airborne ranger, I have to make the jump at five different times," he explained.

The day came for Ron to prove himself. He was in the plane, the door open, the gear strapped onto his body. He knew the procedure was to jump out, count to ten, look up to check that the parachute opened, and then enjoy the flight.

Ron clarified, "It was my turn to make the jump, but I was paralyzed until I felt a hand on back, the strong wind hit my body and I was out of there. There was no sound, perfect silence. And I was thinking to myself 'I must be dead. I did not survive. I am dead and in Heaven. No, I cannot be dead cause I can feel the wind. Oh, I forgot to count and check that my parachute opened."

Ron said he finally looked up and saw that his parachute had indeed opened and heard the distinctive snap indicating everything was engaged.

"That was my first and only jump from an airplane. I must have been crazy to do that!" He laughed.

"Okay, truth now, did you really jump," I asked, seriously, "or were you pushed out?"

Ron was always kind and generous with all that he had, and not just to our little family, but to everyone. When he first joined the Army, he sent a savings bond to his mother, telling her to use it however she needed it. That continued until he retired, twenty-three years later. They did not discuss whether she got it each month or what she did with it. If he knew there was a need, he tried to fill that need. If you needed a coat, just tell Ron. He would give you his. One of his high school students, twenty-five years later was lamenting about her mother's upcoming wedding.

"Sergeant, none of my friends will be there. Will you come?" she had asked.

"Of course, I will come to support you," Ron confirmed. He fussed about it for a week, but when the day came, he put on his dress shirt and a necktie and went to that wedding. He asked me to come with him, but I had a prior engagement.

He said, as he stood next to his student to witness her mother getting married to her female partner, "Your mother looks great!"

The student was ecstatic. Our wedding had been just as memorable.

A Simple Wedding

The wedding was set for the sixth of November in 1971. My brother, Grady, who was working in Louisville, Kentucky, was going to come to Cadiz to give the bride away. Daddy did not plan to attend. One week before the ceremony, Grady called to say that he wasn't coming home because a good friend of his had passed away. The funeral would be on my wedding day. Attending the funeral was important to him because he had never been to a funeral. So he stayed in Louisville and attended the funeral that weekend.

My sister, Jean, had made the arrangements to have a reception at her house after the ceremony. The ceremony would be at my home church, Bloomfield Baptist Church. The marriage service would be officiated by Pastor Darden. My three friends had come from Bowling Green to witness the union. Ron had chosen as his best man a longtime friend, Norman, who lived in Cadiz. My youngest sister, Zora, was my Maid of Honor.

With the exception that Ron was a little late, things went well. I wore a light tan, knit, knee-length dress with short cap sleeves and a short veil. The dress had an open slit at the throat. I had created the ensemble in my clothing class at the university. My brother, Buster, walked me down the aisle and handed me over to Ron. A week later, Grady passed away from a pulmonary embolism at the age of twenty-three. A week after that, we were having his funeral.

After the wedding and the reception, Ron and I went back to Bowling Green, where we booked a room at a hotel. We stayed together for one week. I went back and forth to my classes at the University; I knew I needed to. At the end of the week, I took Ron to the airport in Nashville, and he boarded a plane for Korea. It would be thirteen months before I saw him again. I finished my classes and earned my Bachelors' degree. At the end of the school year, 1972, I moved back to Cadiz to find a job and get to work. I knew it would be a long time before Ron was able to make much money. I was able to find a job that took me almost all the way to the time when my husband would return.

<u>Waiting and Working</u>

That year, 1972, I worked for the Tennessee Valley Authority, which is located about forty-five minutes away. Historically, it used to be in a community called Canton until the federal government bought out all the homeowners, flooded the area and made parks with a lake and resorts. I bought a small car—a standard shift Datsun. I asked my brother, Ollie, to teach me to drive it. We had great fun while he gave me a full week of lessons. It was a decent job with average pay, no benefits, working on a man-made lake. The job had horrible shift hours. I either went in to work my shift in the dark or I finished my shift just in time to drive home in the dark. It was a dangerous forty-five-minute commute each way because of the possibility of crashing into deer as they ran about the heavily wooded compound. The roads were curvy and hard to maneuver, especially at night. I had two other jobs to keep me busy though.

I had a home business job selling home goods. I sold kitchen items and all kinds of items for the home. I learned how to be a salesperson and present myself to others. I was able to draw back onto my earlier speech training, despite thinking those classes were just for fun. I also taught one Science class every morning at Trigg County High School. However, this job did not last long. I let it go when I moved out of the county. The TVA gig was a temporary government job that lasted about nine months. I had turned down the teaching job in the Appalachian Mountain area because I wanted to be available to make a home with Ron and Nick, when Ron returned. I thought it over before I turned it down and chose to be a wife and mother, available for travel.

Chapter 7

FIRST MILITARY MOVES

<u>Temple, Texas</u>

I moved from my parents' home to a house I rented in Hopkinsville to wait for Ron's return from overseas duty in Korea. When he returned, we loaded our furniture and our other few possessions and we set out to Texas in a rented U-Haul. Ollie accompanied us to help with the driving. It was a long trip, but we were young and having fun. We even put my little Datsun in the truck None of the furniture was covered or padded. We really did not know what we were doing—kids in love when we married who grew up together, after we were married. We made a pact, like children and agreed that if we loved each other, we would make our union work.

Ron was stationed at one of the larger military installations in the United States, Fort Hood. My husband had rented an apartment in Temple, Texas, because housing was not available on base. We moved our things in, made a few friends, and got settled. The military installation was a forty-five-minute drive away. Ron made the daily commute. I searched for a job and daycare center that would be open during regular business hours of eight to five. I was pleased to enroll Nick into one that was owned by a Black family. The daycare owner was efficient and caring. I was immensely impressed with the way her staff interacted with the children.

There was a time when I was terribly sick. I had to be off from work and on a complete week of bed rest because of the illness. I could not take care of my son or go to work.

I presented my dilemma to the daycare center workers and was assured that they would take care of my child. The way they handled it was ingenious. The owner, a wonderful Christian woman, sent a car around to pick him up in the morning and they kept him late in the evenings until my husband could pick him up from work. That meant a lot to me.

At this point, I was starting to feel a little homesick. I missed the extra help that I would have gotten from family while raising children. I wanted my sisters and my mama. So, it was a relief that I had chosen a daycare center that could be like family. They often went beyond the normal duty with the children, treating them like their own.

With the childcare situation taken care of, I focused on finding a job. A perfect employment fit presented itself during an interview at Temple Hospital, working as a personnel secretary. It was my job to assist the director of personnel in hiring, greeting the public, and keeping records. It was 1973 and I felt the same anguish I had felt in 1963 when told I had to become a part of integration. Things had not changed much in the Southern states. There were many days when people came into the office to apply for a position or just ask a question, but when they saw me sitting in the outer office, they either had negative comments to make or changed their mind and decided they did not want answers. Sometimes, they did not want an application if they had to get it from a Black person. I was young and naïve and thought that I had left discrimination and biases behind when I left Kentucky. It saddened me to find out that I had not. It actually followed me. Day-to-day life was routine. Sometimes things unexpected happened and had to be dealt with right away. It did add a bit of excitement to the mundane schedule.

I made a few friends with other military wives. There was time to socialize. One of the ladies that I met first was Joanne. She was from Georgia. We were both in our early 20s. I would tease her about her Georgian accent because there were many things that she said I had to ask her to repeat. She was a good sport about her accent, and we became good friends.

She had one son whose name was Sam. We cooked, shared food and recipes, shopped together, and helped with each other's children. She taught me how to cook collard greens. Mama cooked mustard and turnip greens, so I did not know about collards. On weekends we got together with our husbands and children to play games and share stories about the week. We celebrated each other's accomplishments and sympathized with the losses and disappointments. However, three things happened that caused breaks in the monotony.

The first thing, I learned about from the television, after getting home from work one evening. The weather in Texas was usually very hot. The television gave us the news that possibly there was a tornado heading toward our area. This was a night when my husband was working night shift, so he was not home. The wind got very high, and created shrieking, and rumbling sounds and it got scary.

Our apartment was on the second floor. I had experienced a tornado while staying for three weeks in Murray, but this was the first time I had experienced a tornado coming so close. I don't know which one was scarier. Both times, I was responsible for keeping a toddler safe.

Trying to remember the training that I had received when I was in high school, I grabbed a flashlight, some blankets, and bottled water. Taking these items with us, Nick and I went in a bedroom that had no windows and hunkered down in a corner. While the winds howled and torrential rains beat against the building, I held on to my son and waited. And prayed.

As tornadoes are short, this one did not last very long. The winds died down and we were safe. Ron came home later, rushing up the stairs and into the house. He said, "When I saw all the devastation in the neighborhood, with the trees all down and some of the roofs missing on houses, and a few cars turned over, I got very worried. I was scared you were not okay. I'm glad y'all are fine."

"I was scared but could not let Nick how scared I was," I told him.

<u>Bug in my Ear</u>

The second thing happened as I stood by the apartment door early one evening, just after dark. The outside door light was on. Bugs fluttered around the light as I fumbled for my door key. As the door swung inwards, I felt something light on my right ear. I swatted at it and went inside. I went about settling Nick in for bed, then felt something crawling way down deep in my ear.

I screamed, "Ron, I think something is in my ear!"

"What? Is it ear wax?"

As I went in the house I panicked, "No, it's a bug! It flew in while I was unlocking the door! It's making noises and it hurts."

When I screamed louder, he got Q-tips to try and help. He then poured in some Castor oil. Nothing happened, except the noise in my ear increased.

"I need to go to the hospital to get it out!"

He mumbled, "Okay", and agreed reluctantly.

We arranged for Joanne, the downstairs neighbor, to care for Nick. Then we were off to the Temple Hospital. The doctors looked in my ear with an otoscope.

"Yeah, there is a bug in there all right. How did you manage that?" he asked, chuckling. I did not think it was funny. There was a full orchestra in my ear. The doctor tried the ear wash. Nothing. In the meantime, I tried to keep from screaming. The doctor dropped in some warm oil. I lay on my side on the table, waiting for the bug to make its way out. After a few minutes, still nothing happened.

After several minutes of squirming on the table and moaning. Still nothing. No bug making an exit. The doctor used long, thin tweezer-like forceps, to find and extract the noisome creature that was rubbing its legs or wings together creating the rustic, deafening, chirping and pain in my ear. Finally, the doctor was satisfied that no damage had been done to my eardrum. He added in a little bit of soothing oil and I could go home. For several days, I put bits of cotton in my ears, just to make sure that no bugs got in.

Third, on weekends, we went to play at Belton Lake with our friends from the apartment complex. We played games in the park with the children and played in the lake until we could not do it anymore. The best part came when the men grilled hotdogs and hamburgers for everybody. This was my first trip away from home; my first "I'm-on-my-own" move. So far, things were going well. Military life was exciting.

Ron got assigned to a recruiting position in Leesburg, Florida. I was jumping up and down with excitement. I had heard so much about the Sunshine State and could hardly believe I had a chance to live there for a while. We moved from Temple in less than one year.

Beaches, Oranges, and Amusement Parks

When I got to Florida, I was elated. The weather was perfect. It was warm and sunny all the time; one of the places I had dreamed of vacationing in. When we first got to Leesburg, we could not find a place to stay. That was disappointing. We had money but no connections. There had not been enough time before we left Texas to make prior arrangements for living quarters. There were several places that were advertised for rent, until we showed up to apply for the apartment. The white owners looked at us and declared there was no vacancy.

"No vacancy? But we just talked to you."

"It was just rented," they lied.

"But we have an appointment," my husband said.

"No vacancy," they repeated. Some of the landlords just flat-out said, "We don't rent to niggers." That happened several times, in the winter of 1974. It seemed that discrimination was rampant in Florida. Ron and I had decided to take a chance on finding an apartment in Leesburg rather than have Nick and me stay in Texas while he was on the temporary assignment.

We continued to search for a comfortable place, staying weeks in a roadside motel while we looked for a place. We played the tourist card and settled on a resort in the middle of an orange grove called Chalet Village located on the outskirts of Leesburg. It turned out very well for us. My husband had to do a lot of driving, going to recruiting stations, and schools in surrounding towns. Nick and I had time to spend together, getting to know each other. For me, that was a godsend. I felt like I was making up for missing most of the first year of his life when I was in school. For the first time, I could relax and not worry about going to work. I loved living in the tropics.

There were several things to do in the area. Disney World was just one of them and a lot of fun. I always thought I would be afraid of high-flying rides but found it to be a heady experience. My two favorite rides were, and still are, *20,000 Leagues Under the Sea* and *It's a Small World*. Disney World had only been opened since October 1971. This was my first trip to a theme park of its magnitude; I was as excited as a little kid. One of the guys at the radio station and working with the recruiters got tickets for all of us. Tickets were exorbitantly priced at $5.25 for the park entrance tickets and upwards to $6.50 for an eight-ticket coupon book for the rides. Ron, Nick, and I were guests of a guy named Ed and his wife, two of the nicest and unassuming white people that I ever met. We had a wonderful time. There were no long lines to wait in. We could ride one ride more than one time and still have the time to enjoy them all. Everything was bigger than life. The bright colors brought attention to everything and was so impressive I did not know where to look or go first.

The accompanying music boomed over the park, inviting us to enjoy the happiest place on earth. Oversized Mickey and Minnie, in costume, appeared to be in more places than one at the same time. Nick, however, was not impressed, choosing to hide behind me when one of the characters with a gigantic, permanent grin approached him to greet him, wanting to shake his little two-year-old-hand with a huge rubberized one.

In north Florida, at an amusement park in Silver Springs, we saw water-life through glass-bottomed boats and maneuvered paddle boats on muddy rivers. There was a variety of fish and water life under those boats. The foliage was thick surrounding the river. I felt like we were in the jungle in a Tarzan movie. I saw my first alligator, just hanging out at the edge of the river, lounging in the sun. It was about five feet long. But I made sure to keep my distance from the alligator, again, like I was in that Tarzan movie.

Years later, on a trip to Fort Lauderdale, in the swampy backwaters of south Florida, from my seat in a glass bottom-bottomed air boat, I felt the same anxiety while looking at alligators in the swampy waters. In Leesburg, I ate citrus fruit right off the trees. We had no shortage of fresh citrus fruits since we lived in an orange grove. In Kentucky, oranges had been a luxury at our house. We picked these right from the tree and ate the juicy pulp on the spot. We tried all the fruits: the limes, pomegranates, pomelos, lemons, grapefruits and traveled throughout central Florida by car on weekends, whenever Ron was off from work.

We even visited my oldest sister, Neta, and her family in Live Oak, bringing an assortment of fresh fruits for the family. She had been living there about 20 years, but this was the first time I had visited her. I was glad to visit because I had not seen her in a long time. Twelve years older than I am, by the time I was starting to grow up, she was gone from the family home. She lived with her husband and children on their farm, raising vegetables and peanuts. They also raised pigs. The house was set in a grove of trees, hanging with heavy Spanish moss. It was cozy and snug. This was a chance to get acquainted with her and her family. We visited with her several days on the working farm where they lived. Citrus fruits do not grow well in the temperatures that far north, so our gift was appreciated, especially by the children.

Here, I went to the ocean for the first time. The sounds of the crashing waves, the seagulls screeching, and the gentle breeze on my face created a sensation in me akin to being close to the Holy Spirit. I marveled at the strength of the unending horizon and the fact that the water stayed where it was supposed to be. The water came in; the water went back out. Nothing man can do about it. Power of God. It was peaceful and soothing on the beach on the western beach, near Clearwater. I easily imagined myself in my own little beach house, living the tropical life.

Chapter 8

ON THE MOVE

Texas Again

The recruiting assignment lasted about six months. Once the assignment in Leesburg was finished, we were directed to return to Fort Hood. We moved to Killeen to live, just outside of the post. There still were no quarters available for us to live on the base. The apartment that we had in Killeen was appropriate for the small amount of furniture we had. Ron had chosen a two-bedroom apartment that was adequate size. For the first time, I was experiencing military life as a wife and having a family on a military post, even though we did not live on the post. We were right outside the base entrance. Everything that we needed was close by. The downside to this was I did not have a job and Ron was constantly gone. When he was not home, he was on military maneuvers. He worked hard and was advancing quickly through the ranks—attending classes and working on his Associate's degree.

While he was gone, I oversaw the home. Even when he was present, I managed the home and I took pride in keeping it clean, preparing meals, and caring for Nick. I bonded with neighbors and started multiple projects; I managed to keep myself busy with craft projects and sewing. I made a few friends there, but nothing that really lasted. I spent my days with my son, and I got a lot of reading done. But, I was lonely. I had not expected to spend so much time apart from my husband. From the time spent in Temple, I knew how to manage the apartment, make simple, nutritious meals, and manage the budget.

I did not really like Killeen because it was always hot and muggy. We did a little bit of travel away from the post. When Ron did not have work duty, we drove to Austin. While we were in Austin, I shopped in some outdoor malls. This was new for me. On other weekend excursions, I found some wonderful malls in Dallas and in Waco.

One weekend, we crossed the border into Mexico, spending a delightful day in Juarez, trying to absorb a little of the culture buying trinkets. I learned to eat Mexican food. We traveled to Houston where I learned to appreciate beautiful sunsets. Houston is a large city, but I liked the beaches best of all. I think this was the beginning of my love and attachment to white sandy beaches. The beaches were like the ones in Florida, all along on the Gulf of Mexico. The breeze coming off the ocean and into the Gulf makes the beach experience one of pure bliss; a feeling I wanted to cherish.

Military for Me

At one point, I made up my mind to take the test to join the Army. I figured enlisting would solve the problem of being separated from my husband. Ron encouraged me to do so because it also meant more money in the household. I took the exam and passed without having any issues. The next step was to interview with the officer's board. The interview revealed several pieces of information I didn't know. There was no guarantee that a couple would be stationed together. All of that would depend on what slots were available at the different military establishments. I also learned that I would have to find my child a reliable caregiver for the time that I would not be able to care for him myself because of work.

I also found out that the military frowned seriously on enlisted personnel and officers cohabitating. I would be an officer because I already had my Bachelor's degree. That meant that I would outrank my husband. He was working on his degree and did not want to be an officer.

After passing the physical, I made another appointment for the decision as to whether or not I would be accepted. At first, the officer's board said there were too many rules that I would be breaking. The answer they brought back to me was to refuse my admission. The fact that I was female also gave them cause. Females in the military were a rarity in 1974. After the draft ended in 1973, only two percent of military enlisted females were women and eight percent were in the officer corps. I didn't like their answer, so I fought to get in, writing letters and making numerous phone calls.

After a few weeks and another meeting or two, it was decided that I could join the Army. My great-grandfather, born in the mid 1800s, had been an enlisted man. He had been a slave and had been in the service as far back as the Civil War. My father had been in the service. Two of my brothers had served the country, as well. Three of my family members had been to war and I was proud to be joining them in their ranks and to add my service for my country in the military to theirs.

When the day finally came to sign the papers, I suddenly panicked. I was scared. I could not make my hand pick up the pen. At the very last minute, I decided the military was not for me. I wanted to be with my child. I'd already left him once while I finished school and didn't want to leave him for someone else to raise, for indefinite periods of time. I felt badly that I had wasted so much of everyone's time. That morning, I made the decision that my family would always come first. I had stood up for females in the military in a time when changes were necessary, and I took a stand for my son and my future children.

I felt good about what I had done. I had fought for something that I thought was important and I had won. I also realized that I serve my country as part of the support team of military spouses. It is a full-time commitment and requires tremendous tenacity.

Ron's superior officer once said, "The Army did not issue a wife."

The Army is always first and foremost in the officers' minds. The Army is their duty. The Army is their responsibility. The Army is their life. For the ranks of military service, those who take the oath to protect and defend the United States, it is serious, pledging their lives to others.

So, I learned to entertain myself and care for my child. I learned to enjoy the time I spent alone. I read a lot. I sewed a lot. I cooked, tried new foods and recipes. I spent time with my neighbors. We stayed at Fort Hood one year, then it was time to shift, pack up, and move again.

Chapter 9

GOING ABROAD

The Trip

We were going to Europe. Just the idea of living abroad gave me jitters. Ron's next order was a three-year tour of duty in Germany, but he elected do two years, forgoing some of the Army's benefits, like family expenses being paid and housing on the military installation. From the beginning, I was extremely excited about the trip because it was the longest time that I would spend on a plane, as well as my first time out of the country, except for the one day in Mexico. Ron went to Germany ahead of us. He stayed several months and returned home in December. I was glad he was home. We stayed at his mother's house while he was home. I soon found out that I was pregnant again. That was good news, but the timing was off. My baby would be born in a foreign country. I did not want to stay in Kentucky while Ron went back to Germany.

We paid our own way to Germany. Doing so meant we were not entitled to have a car or government quarters or household goods shipped. We had a commercial flight from Nashville, Tennessee, because of its proximity to Cadiz. When we arrived in New York, things were hectic. A winter snowstorm was causing havoc. It was December 1974.

"Our flight is delayed until in the morning." Ron shared his report as he returned from the ticket counter. There were so many people everywhere.

"The airline will not put us up in a hotel room. I already asked." My husband said to me.

I asked him, "So what are we going to do?"

Not being fazed by the chaos around him, he replied, "Let's just find a corner somewhere and stay the night." I was indignant.

"What! You have got to be kidding! No, that's not going to work."

"It's only for a few hours anyway."

"Ron, Let's just go find a room, so we can rest. Nick needs to rest, too. We have a big day tomorrow."

"All right," he said grudgingly. And together we went to ask at the counter about nearby hotels. We found a place, with the airline's help. An airport shuttle took us to a Holiday Inn, practically around the corner. We got up early the next morning, refreshed and ready for the next part of the adventure.

Our flight was approximately eight hours from New York to Frankfurt. De-boarding the plane and finding our luggage was quite an ordeal. It helps to know the language, at least some of it, when traveling in another country. We had to wait for our commuter train to take us to Nuremburg, where we were to spend the night.

While we waited, I needed to use the restroom. I had never been one to favor public restrooms. And this time, all the signs were in German—a language I did not know. The signs for restrooms, however, were international, so I could recognize where they were. Ron pointed me in the right direction. Once I was in the restroom, there was also another person dressed as an attendant. She was responsible for not just making sure the facility was kept clean, but also providing the necessary services. She handed out towels to refresh oneself and offered a variety of toiletries. However, I saw patrons leaving money before they used the restroom. Their gestures indicated I should do the same. I left, agitated, having no money, and told Ron that I still had not used the restroom.

Ron had already been living in Germany for a few months, so he knew how the system worked, but forgot to tell me. I did not think it was funny, yet he got a good laugh out of the situation.

I sat on the train station's bench, with hundreds of people moving around and staring at me, while I had my first emotional meltdown. Afterwards, we went to the Money Exchange counter and exchanged some of our U.S. dollars for German Deutsche Marks. We were set, and I was finally able to use the restroom. But, I still did not what the custom was. Was the attendant there working for tips or for the train station?

Ron decided for us to spend the night in Nuremberg before taking another train to Bamberg. Since Ron chose to only do two years in Germany, instead of three, he was not entitled to housing on the military base and had to find a living space for our family. I was excited about the place he had chosen for us to live for the next two years, especially since the hotel accommodations had been so impressive, with the huge bed and lots of downy coverlets to keep the cold out. The next day, we took a taxicab to our new home on the outer skirts of Bamberg.

<u>Another Home</u>

The place that Ron rented for us was rustic, in a small community nestled among rolling hills. He was stationed in Bamberg, Germany, approximately fifteen miles away. Our efficiency apartment was a place above a garage in the country. From my window, I could see the castles in the distance, the rolling hills, the mountains, the curving highway, and small groups of people who walked along the roadside. Walking was the Germans' way of recreation in the community.

When we first got to the apartment, I walked in and my reaction was a horrified, "Oh No!"

Fifteen stone steps, without a railing, led to the apartment's small hallway entrance. The kitchen consisted of a one burner electric stove, a half size refrigerator, a tiny table cramped in the corner and a little counter space. Across the hall from the kitchen was the bathroom. It had a unique tub with old-fashioned claw feet. The toilet had the chain pull for flushing the toilet. There was a sink in one corner. The tub and the sink were so dirty, I didn't know what color they were. I looked at it and I started to cry.

"Now, what's wrong?" Ron asked.

I said to him, "This is much too dirty. I cannot live here". He put his arms around me to calm me down. Then we went into the other part of the apartment where there was a small living room with a bay of windows and sliding panels to keep the cold out. In one corner, there was a heater that used kerosene. When I saw the kerosene heater, I had flashbacks of my childhood home in Kentucky where the source of heat was a coal-burning stove. I was so not ready for this.

The master bedroom had a huge king size bed, and the mattress was down inside a box-like structure. It was covered with thick, downy coverlets. The closet was not actually a closet, but it was a heavy mahogany wardrobe like the American chifforobe, free standing with two doors and shelves for storing belongings. There was also a dresser with a mirror in that room.

There was no more room for anything else. It struck me as being impossible to do anything other than to go to bed. A second bedroom, which was about the size of a closet, would be Nick's bedroom. The bed folded up into the wall so that when it was folded up there was room to move around and for him to play. It could work, although the apartment was not what I had in mind.

Ron consoled me and agreed that he would clean the place. That was when I learned that he had excellent organization and housekeeping skills. This is one of the things that we chuckle about when we reminisce about our trip to Germany.

"You were such a baby when I brought you there the first time," he teased.

These were the beginnings of new experiences that I had to learn to maneuver. I had to teach myself to survive in a foreign country. Most things were different. We were living apart from the military installation where all things were provided for families. We lived in a village with the German people, not live in one of the modern apartments. The military called it "living on the economy". It was not just the living quarters that were different. The culture was different from the United States. For example, most German people shopped for their food daily. American military, on the other hand, shopped for groceries for a week or two at a time at a commissary stocked with products mostly made in America. Living on base would have been like being at home. Therefore, in Germany there was no need for the large refrigerators that we had in our kitchens in the United States.

The town we lived in was a small village, with some farming done in the neighborhood and some small businesses, as well. Ron paid a soldier who was returning to the United States, one hundred dollars for a 1963 Volkswagen. It proved to be well worth the money. One of the other three military families living in the building had a car also. Fortunately, I had learned to drive on a standard shift. My husband used the car to get to work almost every day. One or two days each week, he would leave the car with me so that I'd have transportation some of the time. If I were running an errand, I checked with the other Army wives to see if they needed anything.

Oftentimes, they needed transportation, as well. When I didn't have the car, I took the bus. The other wives and children and Nick would put on their wintertime gear and we would go to the military post at Bamberg, the dispensary to get immunizations, or sightseeing to get out for a little while. Of course, I could not take all three families at the same time; after all, it was a Volkswagen. They would take turns going with me or they would ride the bus. I could walk to the local meat market to get a small number of items to prepare one or two meals. I also enrolled in a class of conversational German on the base in Bamberg, so I could learn to communicate enough to complete a transaction at the market. I enjoyed the company and soon did not feel so lonely when Ron was working long maneuvers.

Addition to the Family

Our German landlord gave me a big, bulky stroller to use with the new baby, when she found out I was pregnant. We had arrived in Germany just after Christmas. Germany in the wintertime was colder than anything I was used to in the hills of Kentucky. Eight months later, I started to have what I perceived to be labor pains. I was ready to go to the city to get checked out at the dispensary before starting the long drive to Nuremberg for the delivery; I was nervous.

The whole procedure was different. Once the medical personal in Bamberg determined that I was indeed in labor, I was to be transferred by ambulance to the hospital in Nuremberg. We got my four-year-old son settled with the neighbors. The arrangements had been made when I had my last check-up visit. My husband was nervous since he had not been there for the birth of our first child. He had come home on the day that I came home from the hospital.

As I moaned and groaned with the pain, Ron said, "Come on, come on! Let's go!" as he hustled me to the car.

"Where is the hospital bag?" he asked, excitedly, as I wobbled down the stone that had no hand railing. Ron helped me by holding my hand and guiding me down the steps using his body as support.

"The bag! Don't forget the bag," I yelled. He opened the passenger side door and helped me get settled in.

"Where is it?" Ron questioned.

"It is right where we decided it would stay. On the floor next to heater. Please hurry." I whimpered through another pain.

Ron ran quickly back up the stone stairs to get the bag. Running back down the stone stairs, completely out of breath, he jumped in the car, ready to go.

"I got it!", he exclaimed as he put the key in the ignition and started the car. He pulled off the emergency brake, put the car in first gear, eased his left foot off the clutch. The car moved forward.

"Wait. What was that thump?" Then, he realized the car had a flat tire. It was almost the end of August and the weather was already cold. I got out of the car, with my devastated husband helping me, and hobbled back up the stone steps. I waited inside while he changed the tire. Two of the upstairs neighbors came down to keep me company. All the wives who lived there had children. They offered sympathy and comfort. I was glad they were there for me. When the tire was replaced, Ron came back inside to get me.

"Good luck!" they shouted as we all left the house.

Finally, we were off to the dispensary, which was a twenty-minute ride. The attendant on duty completed the perfunctory examination and determined that I needed to be on the way immediately to the hospital. The medics got us into an ambulance, and we were on our way. The driver took the most expedient route, which was the German autobahn, the federal-controlled access highway system. Translated loosely, autobahn means 'federal auto track' or 'motor freeway'. There are no speed limits, which makes it faster but more dangerous. Every time I was on the super-highway, it felt like being on a rollercoaster. Although this ride was no exception, being in an ambulance felt a bit safer.

Despite the setbacks, our baby girl was born healthy and alert, in that German hospital in the town of Nuremberg. However, we had to do all the things that we needed to do and to welcome Alanna into our world with two birth certificates to prove her dual citizenship. Ron had misspelled her name.

"It's okay," he said, "it is just one letter, and her name can be Alonna."

I challenged him, "No, that is not the name I want for her. Her name is Alanna."

It was a challenge to make the change, but Ron stuck with it until we had perfect birth certificates. When I sent a picture of her home, everyone said she looked just like my mother.

As I became more acclimated to my new routine, I was grateful to have the privilege to travel and live in another country. It felt good to be immersed in that culture and find out how other people lived. There was a lot of unusual things to do. Just as the weather started to warm up for spring, one bright sunshiny morning, I threw open the shutters and opened the windows.

"What is that smell?", I thought aloud to myself. It was extremely potent and smelled like feces. The whole neighborhood smelled contaminated; awful enough to make me gag. Closing the windows, I went to check with my upstairs neighbors.

"Oh," Deb explained. "It is time for Frau Mueller to make her garden."

Just that simple. The septic tank had been emptied and spread over the entire backyard. Used as fertilizer, the disgusting smell dissipated after a month or so. None of the wives used the backyard much, anyway.

About two months later, I found a basket of large, plump, red strawberries on my top step. The placement of the gift of strawberries continued throughout the growing and harvesting season. I accepted each basket of strawberries, as did the other wives. When Frau Mueller came (she lived in Munich and came at the end of each month to collect rent), I was careful to thank her in my best broken German, and understood that some secrets must be kept.

There was so much to see, so much to do, and so much to learn. Nick started school while we were there. Because his birthday was in the middle of December, he was able to attend kindergarten at age four. He was bright, learned quickly, was always happy, laughing and interested in the things around him. I worked as a substitute teacher at the American school and participated in the local social activity life, being a member of the parent-teacher association, volunteering to help a teacher. The four military families who lived in the apartment building had been there long before we arrived. My husband knew the other husbands. They had told Ron about the empty apartment situated above the garage.

As we became friends, we babysat for each other. This allowed us to do things without our children, but knowing they were safe, we could go places in other parts of Europe. All three wives took turns with Deb and Rich's baby while they went on a four-day holiday to France. Rhonda and Millie were content with staying home. They didn't take any trips while I was there. I, on the other hand, planned as many trips as I could squeeze into our time in Bavaria.

The men were busy on maneuvers or duty and had little time for family. It was up to the military wives to make family life pleasant. Deb and Rich were the youngest couple in the building. Their daughter was the youngest child among us, and she was born in Germany. Sometimes, their daughter cried all night, sometimes all day. None of us could get her to stop crying either. When Deb and her husband returned from the trip to France, they took her to a specialist for a hearing evaluation. They had already tried everything else. The doctors could not find anything amiss. It remained a mystery.

All Aboard the Train

After Alanna was born, Ron and I took a train trip to Austria, Switzerland, Bergkirchen, Munich, and Dachau. I could hardly enjoy the first part of the train trip because I was anxious and having a hard time relaxing. The train was comfortable. People on the train were friendly and cheerful. I kept thinking that I might fall asleep, miss our stop and end up beyond the checkpoint at the border that indicated we had entered Czechoslovakia. I had read enough about the Nazi Germans being on rampage in The Diary of Ann Frank to know that if we found ourselves in this land-locked country, we would likely be in big trouble. Until 1989, this was a communist country, working with Russia, called USSR. Its politics were in opposition to those of the capitalist Western Bloc, which included the United States, during the Cold War.

We had all the proper identification. I was partly uneasy because of the language barrier and partly because it was a dismal place, from what I saw as we got closer to the border.

My basic course in conversational German served me well at the market, but not well enough in our travels. Whenever Ron's work schedule permitted, we saw most of the surrounding towns in the southern part of Germany, called Bavaria, and left Nick and Alanna with the upstairs wives for a few days. We packed a bag and took the train first to a salt mine near Austria. We got in line to take the tour through the mine. It was required that we wear protective clothing to enter the mine. We dressed up in workman's gear to learn how salt was mined. This uniform included coveralls of a heavy denim-like fabric, a snug fitting cap made of the same material, gloves, and shoe covers.

The uniform was all in a drab gray. It reminded me of the coal mining in the hills of Western Kentucky and the state of Virginia. It was interesting to see the salt being mined and prepared for use. Some of it was used in spas, while some was used in making seasoning for foods. Salt was mined to be used to make several commercial products, such as the preservation of meats and cosmetic products. I purchased a little box of salt squares as my souvenir. We went back to the train station for the next stop on our list: Switzerland.

Switzerland was cold and snowy. For the sake of trying new things, we had decided to try our stamina and aptitude with skiing. First, we got some basic instruction from an attendant. Step one was to get the skis on with the bindings to keep our rented skis attached to our boots, ski and still be standing up. Step two meant you had the ski poles (or ski sticks) in your hands. We got on the ski lift and got off on the Blue Run, the run for beginners. I looked down the snowy hillside at the amateur run, pushed off with my sticks and fell flat on my face. Ron did his take-off to help me, tripped over my body and went tumbling downhill in a flurry of newly fallen snow. I gave it a few more tries.

Downhill…downhill, downhill, I was doing it. Then, just as quickly, the inside binding slipped off. I did another face down in the snow move and played in the snow awhile longer before I gave up. That was the extent of my skiing.

I got out of skis and went inside the hut to rest. It was exhilarating. My husband fared better than I did and got a couple of good partial runs. It had tired us both out. We looked at each other with a big grin and burst out laughing.

I said, "That was fun. Now I'm hungry. Let's go eat." We got back on the ski lift to return to the clubhouse. We gave up. There were too many places that we could end up with broken bones or displaced joints.

Bergkirchen was near the town of Dachau. I suppose it would have been different altogether in the spring because there would be lots of plants, blooming to brighten the place up. We did a lot of talking and walking. We made a trip to a national museum that housed the German Concentration camp. This one was called Dachau.

The concentration camp consisted of stonewall buildings with bars that had housed the prisoners of the Third Reich army captured under the General Adolph Hitler's regime of dictatorship from 1933 to 1945. This was the start of World War II. The trains that had transported the Jewish descendants were there. The life-like mannequins wore the striped prison uniforms, and there were pictures of hundreds of bodies piled together for termination and gigantic kilns for extermination of what became known as the Holocaust. The display showed hundreds of bones to emphasize the horrible dehumanization and deaths of hundreds of thousands of innocent people. It made me realize how tragic things can get when people don't take a stand against wrong actions before they get out of hand. I was encouraged to use my voice against bullies. My voice was just as important as the next person. I had read the historical accounts of the Holocaust, but I had not paralleled it to the experiences of my ancestors during the time when the slavery industry flourished in the United States. Since that time, I have been to the local Florida Holocaust Museum in St. Petersburg, Florida.

The depictions in the stories and pictures there are the same. Being there, walking through the maze of human degradation and studying the displays brought the same feeling of sadness, horror, repulsion, and fear that I had experienced when I walked through the gate and under the arrangement of human bones, hanging from it in Dachau. I had not equated it with the experiences I could have had in my hometown in my youth. But, maybe they are the same. The fear that shuddered through my body was brought on with the knowledge that it could happen again. It almost happened after slavery when civil rights were withheld from millions of 'Colored' or 'Negro' descendants. Things like a proper seat on a bus, eating in restaurants, and the acquisition of voting rights and the right to equal education. Fortunately, someone stepped up to declare the injustice that was being done and demanded changes be made. People, like the Civil Rights leaders in the 1950s and 60s helped to restore rights and liberties. In my recent memory bank, Blacks or African-American (as we are called and listed on official forms) people are still being discriminated against in the lives of women, alternate life choices, education systems, court, politics, healthcare, police profiling. Some progress has been made in the political arena, with the election of two African Americans, President Obama (2008) and Vice President Harris (2020) to the two highest positions in the country.

Experiencing the Culture

There were many things in the German culture that were different from what I was used to. One of the things was the food. A salad, for instance, does not include crisp lettuce like in the United States. My salad was made with wilted greens with a hot dressing poured over it. It was rather tasty but still surprising. Bars were popular in each neighborhood. The tavern was a friendly place to meet, greet, and hang out with friends. Beer was the most popular beverage for breakfast lunch, dinner, and in-between times. I was told that Germans do not drink much water. After a while, I came to believe that. There was a pub in our neighborhood within walking distance, and we went there often.

It was usual for one of the neighbors to offer to buy us a beverage, usually beer. A popular food choice was the Wiener schnitzel. It was made of cubed veal or pork cutlet, with cheese rolled, breaded, and deep fried. That was the one thing that we all loved to eat.

If we went out, that was what we ordered. We could pronounce it, and we liked it. Bratwurst and sauerkraut, two typical German foods, were popular at outdoor food booths as well as on pub menus. They were often served on a hard bun. Add some mustard and it was quite good; add a beer to that and you had an excellent meal. There were many year-round festivals held in the towns. Germany was the first time I went to a real circus with animals, clowns, acrobats, and all the many people inside The Big Top. We had gotten tickets with seats under the Big Top tent. I had no idea that a true circus involved so many intricate things. My family and I were not chosen to participate in any of the activities, but we were a minority in that group. I found that in the intermingling with the locals there was an undercurrent of racism there, too. But, perhaps, it was only curiosity.

I was asked often when having eaten at the neighborhood tavern, "How do you live alongside people who enslaved you?"

Many locals did not like Americans, white or Black. They were accustomed to using the word 'Negro' when referring to us. There were some mixed couples and few children who looked like us. This observation was made when I substituted for teachers in the school system. My German neighbors observed several holidays, some religious. The Germans in our neighborhood were Catholics. They followed their holidays faithfully. My first experience with neighbors observing a religious holiday was when I put my laundry on the clothesline on a Sunday morning.

One of my German neighbors knocked on my door and proceeded to tell me, in German of course, that one did not leave laundry on the line on a Holy Day. To be sure that I understood what she meant, she indicated that I was to follow her down my steps, out to the clothesline and helped me take the clothes off the line. The neighbor was adamant and piercingly unkind. From that point on, I tried to obey the rules that they observed by imitating what they did.

On one evening, near the end of October, adults walked around the neighborhood with their children. Everyone who participated, including the adults, were dressed in gaily-colored costumes. They knocked on doors, asked for treats, sang and chanted as they canvassed the area for candies, cakes, and toys. Their parade culminated at the neighborhood pub. My German neighbors also participated in an annual festival called Oktoberfest—a festival that went on in all the communities with beer, shooting competitions, parades, dancing, and fun.

Oktoberfest does not officially start until the Lord Mayor in Munich taps the first keg and shouts for the festival to begin. Then the mad dash to the tents to score the first beer begins. It seemed as if the whole country celebrated.

Walking was not only a means to get to a short destination, but it was also a part of the German culture. It was common to see a German man walking along the countryside carrying a walking stick and wearing the traditional outfit of leather trousers that end just below the knee with suspenders. Women wore a dress with a bodice, a blouse, a full skirt, and an apron. These outfits were worn during festivals and carnivals. Additionally, I found cleanliness to be important. After having been in New York City, Germany was the cleanest city that I had ever seen.

Housekeepers kept their homes spotless and showed them off. It was customary (especially in the Netherlands) for citizens to keep their curtains open so that passersby could see that their windows were clean, and their house was immaculate. They also kept the area on the street around their house clean. I watched them sweep their street and I marveled at such discipline.

We did not entertain much, but we did make friends with a few people who entertained us in their home and vice versa. The whole experience in Germany was as if I had gone back in time when things moved in a slower pace, where people were more caring and willing to help whenever needed. The walk to the meat market was a pleasure trip, a time to catch up with neighborhood talk. People only shopped a couple of days each week, so I did too. The people I met along the way were always friendly and helpful. I ordered the items I needed in my broken German. If there was a problem, someone was usually there who would help me. If someone was there who spoke English, that made it easier. Broken

German plus broken English together made for understanding and an appreciation for each other.

I loved that I could look out my window and see one of the neighboring castles in the distance. It stood high up on a mountainous hill with its many windows, overlooking the valley below. There were towers and turrets that reached toward the sky. One sunny afternoon, we visited that castle, which was open to the public. This castle was empty. There was a drawbridge with running water under it at the entrance. It was fascinating looking at the way things used to be, and the way people used to live many years ago. The castle grounds were neatly kept. Inside the castle, past generations could be imagined. Other castles in the nearby area were refurbished into country homes, called manors. I marveled at all of the history that was documented.

A Trip Alone

I visited the Netherlands on a bus trip sponsored by one of the organizations on the military base. I went without my family and was assigned a roommate. I had to make new friends quickly. The hotel room was small, but we were only there for a few nights, so it was not a problem. The only problem was that it was early spring during a historically hot season, and there was no air conditioning in most buildings. Even the Germans, who were used to having no air conditioning, were hot. Some businesses, like restaurants, and other proprietors put up large signs in front of their establishment advertising cold air. These places were packed with patrons.

This bus trip was my chance to see Amsterdam, which was interesting to me as I had read about Jewish in Germany, whom Hitler persecuted during World War II. This capital city was known for its elaborate system of canals. I wanted to see the place where Anne Frank lived and wrote a diary to commemorate her struggle to stay alive. I took the tour to the house, crossing the canals to do so. I tried to remember parts from *The Diary of a Young Girl*, about how she hid in the walls of the house to keep from being found and destroyed by Hitler's army. I tried to imagine how lonely and afraid she must have been. The historic houses were narrow and characterized with many gables. They were impressive with tall stately towers. Homes were large and built close together and, in some areas, each building was given a vibrant color, like red, green or purple, alternating the colors on the buildings. I observed this as I walked along the Canal Singel.

While in Amsterdam, I visited many museums and historical sites. The Van Gogh Museum, in the museum district, housed many distinguished artists' work. It broke my heart to see much of this art had been destroyed or stolen during the war, but I was still glad to be there, to experience a little bit of history for myself. I purchased a small oil painting of the colorful houses on the canal before the war destroyed so many of them.

Amsterdam was not all history, buildings, and art. Of particular interest was the red-light district. In this district, ladies of the evening would advertise and promote their services. The ladies would be dressed in enticing regalia and makeup, sitting in their rooms with the windows open. The red lights were on in the background if they were not servicing a client. There is a whole section of streets with ladies lounging in their open windows. Having completed the Netherlands trip alone, I was proud of myself. I was back home to contemplate better ways to care for my children.

Single Parenting

Parenting is an art and I was learning to master it. Nick attended the American Elementary School for the American children of military and government workers' children. One of the other couples in our building had a child who was the same age. Nick and the neighbors' child became friends in kindergarten. On one occasion, parents were invited to the school for a special program, such as lessons given in dental hygiene.

I was pleasantly surprised to see my baby walk out onto the stage to receive a first-place award for dental flossing. He had earned his very first school award. I was so proud of him. It was a good thing and to my knowledge, from then to becoming a man, he never had a cavity. I also remember giving him his first spanking because he was playing in the street. Our apartment was situated in a deep curve. Drivers often ignored the posted speed limit, so it was not a safe place for children to play. He got his first spanking for being too close to the street. It was not unusual for me to wake up in the middle of the night to find the kerosene heater had just stopped working. It was bothersome, antiquated. And I didn't know how to operate it.

Most of the time, we were on our own. Ron's work duty while in Germany, many times, was to be on maneuvers. This required him to be away from the home for weeks and sometimes a month at a time, sleeping outdoors in the woods and working with only what he could carry on his back. I thought we had it bad, but at least, we were inside.

Consequently, I was in charge of our two children and the apartment. If I woke up and had no heat, then I piled on more covers and we all snuggled in together. But, it was still cold. Fortunately, there was another source of heat we could use in emergencies. We turned on the stove in the kitchen. That helped to take away enough of the cold for us not to freeze to death. Then, the next thing to do was to contact Frau. Other times, we woke up to a smoke-filled house. I would open the windows and wait for the smoke to dissipate, then close the windows, stoke up the kerosene stove and hope for the best. It was not an ideal situation. The windows in the apartment were made of thick, double-paned glass. There were times when it was so cold, I packed everybody up and we went to one of the neighbors' houses. We stayed with friends until we could contact Frau. Much of the time in Germany, I felt like a single parent, as I had been before leaving Kentucky.

After two winters, Ron returned with news of our next destination. We were headed back to the United States. I had missed being at home, and home to me still meant being in Kentucky. I thought that was where we were headed and, sure enough, that is where we landed. My hometown of Cadiz was only thirty miles away. I would be close to my family and could visit as often as I wanted. Ron never asked me where I should live, but that was okay. I would have followed him anywhere. I was on an adventure. Again, he chose not to do military housing.

I left Germany before Ron left, with ten-month-old Alanna and five-year-old Nick. I had explicit instructions of what to do once I was back in the States: I was to find a place for us to live near Fort Campbell, the place Ron had tried to get assigned to ever since he'd joined the service in 1969. There were no duty slots for his job assignment at Fort Campbell, previously. But now, he would finally be stationed there. I was to get a place for us that was bigger than our Germany apartment.

Chapter 10

HOME TO KENTUCKY

The Trip Back

The children and I traveled from Bamberg to Frankfurt and boarded a huge, luxurious German plane, Lufthansa Airlines. Fearing the consequence of having to find a lost child, I devised a way to keep up with a toddler and a five-year-old on such a long trip. I carried Alanna in the same back carrier that I had used when she was an infant. Instead of being on my chest, she dangled close to me in a backpack-like harness. Nick and I were connected by a scarf, which could give him up to three feet of wiggle room. I also had necessary emergency travel items in a large bag in my other hand. On the plane, my daughter, smiling and grinning at all the passengers, was passed from one to the other of them as she toddled around in the aisle of the compartment. The airplane was composed of rows that had five seats on each row. The aisles were wide. Breakfast and lunch were served.

The attendants gave the children special service, providing toys, things to color, or extra animal cracker snacks, with juice. One of the attendants took the children on a tour of the plane. The whole process of getting off one plane and onto the other was stressful. We eventually landed at the John F. Kennedy International Airport in New York. The airport was crowded, but we had no trouble making the connection to Nashville, Tennessee, where I rented a car for the two- hour drive to Cadiz. Even though it was crowded, strangers were helpful. One man helped to get our luggage off the carousel.

My children were well-behaved and did not cause any scenes. We were on our way to visit relatives in Cadiz, Kentucky.

When I hugged my mama, it felt like a tall glass of refreshing iced tea. It was so good to be back with my family, neighbors, and friends. The word was out that we were back. Everyone came over to visit.

Mama and Daddy looked good, healthy, and were jovial. And I had come back with an addition to the family. Of course, they had not seen Alanna, who was not exactly a baby anymore, but a rambunctious toddler, basking in all the attention. She was walking and talking. She talked a lot and had an exceptionally good command of the English language. I think it was a case of love at first sight between her and both sets of grandparents. Friends and neighbors came over.

Mama and Jean made some food and we celebrated! We stayed at my mother's house while I searched for a home. I had not realized how much I missed my family for those twenty months or so.

Home Shopping

Our reunion was gratifying and I was glad to be home. At the first of the week, I went to a realtor to search for and to look at rental houses. I became quickly discouraged with the rental prospects. The first realtor I talked to did not seem very interested in renting a house to me. He showed me houses that were dilapidated, filled with unpleasant doggy smells, lawns were unkempt and in run-down neighborhoods. The landlords also wanted more money for rent than it seemed worthwhile.

The second attempt at house-hunting started out slowly, as well. I immediately told the guy that I did not need his services. Beginning to feel frustrated after just two days, I was driving along the main road, Fort Campbell Boulevard, when a red and white Century 21 Realtor sign caught my attention. I turned the car around and pulled into the parking lot. I explained to Paul, the realtor, what I wanted to rent. He took me around to several townhouses and though they were nice, the rent was out of my price point and did not feel right. I guess that was a woman's intuition. At the end of the day, I still had no home. I went back to Mama's house.

The next day, I set out to educate myself about buying a house. I walked into Paul's office early that morning, hoping he did not already have a client.

I said to him, "What, exactly, does it take to buy a house?"

Paul just looked at me, laughed and replied, "Money."

"Very funny, but I want to buy a house. What do I need to do?"

Paul explained the intricacies of shopping for and buying a house.

"So, basically, I need money for a down payment, maybe, closing costs and moving in expenses. I need our credit rating, which you can get and my husband's power of attorney, which I have, and his signature on the contract papers. Right?"

Paul nodded. I made an appointment for the next day to begin the paperwork. I called Ron, still in Germany, to tell him that he was about to buy a house. Then, I celebrated with myself.

Back at my Mama's house, I found Jean there. I was still so excited as I relayed what had happed the past few days. Jean gave me the telephone number for Bobe, the widow of a former Pastor of our church. She lived in Clarksville, but on the outskirts of the city. I called her and she agreed to meet me to show me the various neighborhoods that I might like. I was looking for a quiet, racially-mixed neighborhood, located near integrated schools with good reports, other children in the vicinity and places for the children to play. I wanted to be close to the military facility. When I got to Fort Campbell, I contacted Bobe, who I had not seen in many years. She helped me with the details of a buying a house. She knew her way around the area because she lived nearby. I decided on buying a house because it was more economical to buy one than to pay more for a rented house.

Bobe chose a different realtor to help me work through the process. I had to call Ron twice about financing. I had no idea when I started to buy a house that it would be so easy, with all the necessary proponents in place. With the legal paperwork, I was able to act in my husband's stead. I realized how much trust he had placed in me to do this. We set up a house in a growing neighborhood that was close to the military base. The elementary school was a little more than a mile away so Nick would have to ride a bus from the neighborhood. There were other children in the neighborhood, who would also be taking the bus to that school.

Our little bit of furniture looked lost in the space we were now living in. I didn't have more, so we made do with what we had. The house met all my expectations. There was plenty of room: the required three bedrooms, two baths, living and dining area, a large kitchen, and a family room that faced a huge backyard. There was a garage with space for a washer and dryer. The driveway was paved. The first two years that we lived there, there was no furniture in the living room. The sofa and chair that we owned, I put in the family room with the TV. There were several other military families who lived in the area, so we felt right at home. This time, we were only a mile and a half away from the military base. Living that close allowed us to do our shopping on base and to use the other facilities available to all military; the added "perks" of grocery commissary, department store, and movie theater for military families. We had not had these in our German community. They were available to me but I had to travel to Bamberg to use them. The huge backyard would haunt me when it needed to be mowed every week during the summers. But it was a fantastic place for the neighborhood children to meet for ball games.

I, as Mama had done for my brother, sisters and me, made sure to have plenty of homemade cookies and Kool-Aid. We lived on the state line between Kentucky and Tennessee. It was a great place to be because the area was being developed so quickly. Clarksville, Tennessee, was booming as was Hopkinsville, Kentucky, to the west of the base.

Chapter 11

GETTING ESTABLISHED

Working Years

The family needed a car. While we were getting established, I borrowed one from my brother-in-law, Julius. Eventually, I bought a car because I needed to get a job. I bought the car after I was hired at Christian County School System in 1977 as one of their three home economics teachers at the high school level. I had found a reliable babysitter, Rita, to watch my children while I worked. Rita lived around the corner from us in another subdivision. She, too, was a motherly, military wife, who did not work. My job was an easy twenty-five-minute drive from our house to the high school.

We were settling in. I was trying to juggle a toddler and a six-year-old with a full-time job and keeping house. I knew I could do it. Ron's first call when he landed in Nashville was hilarious to me.

"Where does my family live?" he asked. To this day, I still chuckle about his question. Again, he dropped in and became a part of our family until it was time to pack up again.

Things were going well. I think our family was happy. I taught for two years, but I lacked confidence as an educator and teaching high school students was challenging. I decided at the end of the second year that it was not for me. At one point, on a rainy day, I gave an assignment from the book.

"We don't have any books, Mrs. Curlred."
"They were here on the shelf a minute ago."
Everyone laughed and looked toward Peter.

"Peter, do you know anything about the books?" I asked.

"No ma'am. But I see some words out the window," he said. The whole class laughed. I walked over, looked out the window and I saw, on the ground, in the pouring rain, our precious textbooks.

"All right," I said in my best teacher voice, "shall we draw straws to see who goes out in the rain to get our books?" No laughter, this time. I struggled because I was hardly older than they were and they expected us to be "friends." On impulse, I did something that I had not done before. I gave myself a break and worked until the end of the term, then I resigned. I was able to justify my decision since I did not like teaching. In my mind, there was way too much work for the money and lack of gratitude that you got for that work.

I stayed home for a while with the children, but after a short time, decided that I needed something to do for me.

I had liked teaching Sunday school in my church when I was a teenager, all those years ago. That was fine. But it was only for an hour once a week. I never intended to be a teacher. I had wanted to do something else with my life. I wanted to do something with words. Quitting that teaching job showed me that I needed to rethink my adult life goals. Things did not always go the way I thought they should go. I was educated and trained to be a teacher. I wanted to be that person, just more professional. I wanted to earn the respect of the students. I realized that students react to what they see in the teacher; they could sense the absence of my self-confidence. My mind muddled it over.

One of the teachers at my high school site invited me to a cosmetics home sales party. On a whim, I went. It was not what I expected. I had chosen to go because I needed a social outing that provided me an evening of activity and fun.

When I arrived, one of the first questions was "Is there anyone here who would like to do what I do? Just pay attention and if you still think you might want to give this a try, we can talk afterward. Okay?"

Barb, hosting the gathering, replied, "Of course."

"Yes!" I almost shouted.

I always made my own decisions about my life and my money. I did not have to ask my husband if I thought selling cosmetics was best for me. I became a part of her sales force almost immediately. Many of the characteristics that I needed for teaching, I learned in the training for sales. Barb, my mentor, taught me so many things that helped me grow. I learned how to dress in business-like attire, opting for a dark suit with skirts and flattering blouses in deep blues, reds and greens, low-heeled comfortable dress shoes, to relate to people, to talk to people professionally, to smile, to be confident, and to always put my best foot forward, even when not feeling it. I learned the power of positive thinking, to tell myself what I needed to hear. I loved my new self.

By 1979, I was growing into the person that I wanted to be. I did well in the home sales business, making part of our house into an office and display area. After a few more years, I made the necessary adjustment to enter the education field again. When I left Western Kentucky, I left as a certified teacher for grades 6-12. I had completed my internship as part of that process for the Bachelor's degree. And now, I had gained self-confidence. I was ready.

I was working as an independent beauty consultant, making my own money and managing my family. Meanwhile, Nick had gotten interested in playing baseball. I signed him up for Little League play. He loved playing catcher. He was good at it and made the All-Star Team each summer. That meant traveling around the county for the extended season. He continued to play baseball until he got to high school. Then, he switched to football with the same passion he'd had for baseball, so I fit that into my routine.

All Alone

Things came to a screeching halt when I discovered I was pregnant again in the fall of 1979. I had not decided ahead of time how many children I would have, but when I discovered I was pregnant with number three, I knew that would be the final number.

"This would be a great time for me to go back to school," I thought. "I need to get a Master's degree and this is a good time to do that." The Kentucky teachers' certificate is good only for ten years. Then, you must have your Master's.

As I was pondering these things, Ron left for another duty assignment at Ft. Leonard Wood, Missouri. I was four months pregnant. The rest of the family stayed in Kentucky. That is when I knew our marriage was in trouble. I was left alone to handle family, house and pregnancy. That did not seem right or fair when it was not necessary. Ron had some other options, and he made the choice to leave us there. So, while waiting for birth and at the same time, waiting for Ron to come for us, I was accepted into and attended Austin Peay State University. Austin Peay had the Master's program in secondary education with a minor in Special Education that I desired. Going to this university was ideal because all active-duty military's family member's classes were free. I extended the class load that I was taking to get the degree in the shortest time possible.

An interesting offer of a part-time teaching job in Clarksville became available as the traveling home economics teacher, with one class being special education students. It was something which fit into my already busy schedule. So, I took the job. I was teaching during the daytime and was a part-time student in the evenings. That job did not last long. A special education student's parent insisted that I said something inappropriate to the students. It caused a bit of a stir, but it was not anything that could be proven. The whole incident, however, did leave me stressed out and alone. When the article came out in the local newspaper, I was very upset and taken aback. This couldn't be happening to me. The school system offered no support. They asked me to produce the offending literature. I did. It was a pamphlet from their County Health Department. The administration had not told me to use the information, but I thought it was a good resource. Nevertheless, the county did not hire me back for the next year.

I thought the whole incident was appalling and did not want to deal with it alone. I missed Ron and wanted to share it with him, other than on the phone. I needed his physical support. I hoped that things were going to be all right. I wanted him to put his arms around me and tell me that the bad things would be all right. He chose to stay at Ft. Leonard Wood. That was the maddening part. We were there too long without him. Even though, I don't like to admit it, it's true.

I became a full-time student, and it took me one year to get a Master's degree. I had worked hard for it. The college was located ten miles from our house. I had to travel around the county to observe case studies at the schools that had special programs in what was called Special Education. APSU had two or three floors but no elevators. I had climbed the stairs so many times to get where I needed to be that by the time I'd earned the degree, thirteen days before our third child, Dewayne, was born, I hardly wanted to walk across the stage to get it. At eight and a half months pregnant, I asked

APSU to hold the degree for me. It had been a busy year. While I was pregnant, I had earned my Masters' degree, held down a full-time and a part-time job with my cosmetics business, and continued to manage the family and home.

There were the children and me on one hand, and on the other hand, there was Ron. We were not a functioning very well as a family. Was it because he was seldom home? Was is it because I was bored? Was it because I saw my life passing in front of my eyes and I was not accomplishing the things that I wanted? What was it that was making me unhappy? Why was I dissatisfied? Was it the natural feelings of being at the end of a pregnancy? I pondered these things and tried to tell Ron how I felt unloved and neglected. But he was extremely busy with his job and new friends.

The Day the Water Broke

My neighborhood was quiet the morning I went into labor with Dewayne. It was hot that day for mid-June. While I walked through the house tidying up the disorder the children had left, crossing the family room, I felt my water break. I knew I could go into labor at any time, from that point. I was home alone, with the children. My hospital bag was packed and ready to go. I had hoped when the time came, I would be able to drive myself to the hospital. Most of my neighbors worked during the day, but I called them anyway to ask for a ride to the hospital for delivery. No one was available. I knew I was in labor.

I called my neighbor, Willie Mae. She and her husband, Bew, were home. Both were teachers. Willie Mae and I were friends. She had agreed to mind the children, when the time came for me to deliver. Bew agreed to drive me to the hospital in Hopkinsville. That was fine, and I was relieved that he was willing to take me. I didn't know who was the more nervous of the two of us. He talked constantly, but he got me there safely. Willie Mae agreed to care for Nick and Alanna while I was hospitalized. My family also came to the rescue. Jean and my mother, along with my mother-in-law assisted me with household duties. They cheerfully dug in, assisting me with the children. Jean worked and had her own house to manage. I was glad they were there. After a week, they would leave. And I was on my own to manage my children.

I thought I would be home soon, but there was a misunderstanding between the doctor and me. With my husband gone, I thought I had made it clear that I was to have a tubal ligation after the birth of the baby. The doctor informed me that my husband would have to sign papers for that to happen. I was livid. Was this my body or my husband's? Ron wasn't even in the state.

I boldly insisted, "I am staying until my tubes are tied."

I stayed one extra day. Ron was there by that time. I don't know whether he actually gave his signature or if they finally listened to me. Ron didn't have the right to make that decision. For that reason, I stood my ground. My body. My babies. My decision. We were at Fort Campbell much longer after that.

<u>Mysterious Sounds in the Night</u>

Dewayne was two years old and we had lived in the same Kentucky house for almost seven years, longer than I had lived anywhere since leaving my father's house. One dark night, as I lay in bed ready to sleep, I heard a kind of moaning, high-pitched crying sound.

"Oh my," I thought. "What is that?" I listened intently. "Somebody left their baby in my backyard!"

I waited and listened. I imagined all kinds of things and I was afraid. My children were all asleep. I got out of bed, put on warm clothing, grabbed a flashlight, and went out to see what was causing the noise. I shined the light all around. I even attempted to look in the small crawl space under my bedroom. Nothing. Back into my bed, more of the moaning immediately started again.

I went back outside, determined to find a wild animal caught in something.

"That's it." I told myself. I went to bed and finally managed to sleep. In the morning, I related the incident to one of my neighbors.

"Oh, that's more than likely one of our cats under your house", the next-door neighbor laughingly told me. "I am so sorry the cat kept you awake last night."

The next day, I covered that opening. I did not need pets in my life.

Chapter 12

ON THE MOVE AGAIN

A Belated Honeymoon

My husband and I had not had a romantic time together when we married. This was an ideal time to do it. We were moving from Kentucky to Missouri and left the children in Cadiz for our week on the road. Our first road trip was to the city of beaches, casinos, and boardwalks. I knew we would embark on many more road trips, but this one was special.

Ron was delighted to be going to Atlantic City, New Jersey. He was, and is, enthralled by anything related to Al Capone and gangster movies reflecting times in the thirties and forties. The hotel was elegant with its gold trimming, huge vaults of fragrant flowers, flashing lights, sounds of clanging and dropping of coins, and smoke-filled rooms. People rushing from one game to the next, in the casino. We had purchased a few packages and shopped at an outlet mall. I bought a boom box for Nick. We had the valet park the car and left our newly acquired packages inside.

When we departed, our packages were gone. Lesson learned. All of our furniture had been shipped to our next station, our Kentucky house signed over to a property management company, and our children were waiting to be picked up to go to our new house in Missouri.

Home at Fort Lost in the Woods

Ron had come home to take us back to our new home in Fort Leonard Wood, Missouri. We were traveling by car, in the Cadillac that had been purchased in Kentucky when we were there. This Army post, jokingly called Fort Lost in the Woods, is located about 150 miles West of St. Louis. From St. Louis to Fort Wood, we experienced a desolate part of the United States. This was the first time I had been West of the Mississippi River. I was excited to be making the trip and seeing new things.

"Look at that huge 'thingy' up there in the sky," one of the children said, pointing toward the famous 632-foot Gateway Arch that looms over downtown St. Louis and can be seen from miles away, when entering the city.

We stopped downtown and Ron led us on a guided tour, including a trip up to the apex of the arch. We looked down over the city, amazed at the clarity of the city, towns, and farms in the distance, then strolled on the Riverwalk, enjoying the sunny day, and anticipating the last four-hour drive before we reached our new home.

This time, we would live in the military quarters on the base. We had not done that before, but I still had to get everything ready to move. Ron had done the procedural work of getting us set up for the four-year assignment. He had already served two of his four years while we were still in Kentucky. This meant we were to be in Missouri for two years.

When the military moves your household, it is easier. Ron set up a date for the moving company to come and pack up our things. They did all the work and packed everything. I once saw a packer wrap chicken bones left on the table. I only needed to protect my valuables. I hand packed and carried in the car the German crystal items I had collected while there. The moving company takes your household goods to the next place. Then they unload boxes and place furniture, put beds together and leave the rest to the family. The real work is on the unloading end of the move for the family. Unwrapping kitchen ware, getting everything washed, and put away, means you are almost finished.

The military housing there was large and comfortable. I spent a lot of time getting home set up, again, and one of the next-door neighbors came to help. She and her husband had three girls. We became good friends for the duration of the assignment. She helped me with my children, babysitting when I began teaching. They moved away before we did. We did not maintain contact. It is often that way with other military families you meet—hard to keep in touch with people you may probably never see again.

We moved into a two-story duplex on the side of a steep hill in 1982. The house had four bedrooms and three bathrooms. The master bedroom was nestled in on the first level, facing the angled driveway with its own entry doorway. Our heavy, dark oak bedroom set, with its king- sized bed fit, didn't leave much room to move around. A small bathroom with tub and shower duo served our needs adequately. Dining room, a large kitchen and a small living room made up the first floor of our new home. We loved the house. Nick, exercising first-born privileged chose the bedroom on the back side that had two windows.

Alanna chose next, complaining all the while. "Mom, I should have got first pick. I am the only girl," she whined.

The smallest room would be a family room or playroom. And now, the dilemma, where to sleep two- year-old, Dewayne.

Confidently, I approached Nick, "How would you mind if I put a crib-bed over in that corner of your room?"

"Aww Mom, do I have to? Can't you put him in with Alanna?" he protested.

"Look, if he sleeps in here, all of you have space in this other room to bring your friends, to play your games, and watch television."

"What if I have friends over for the night? Mom, he's a baby!"

"Okay, how about you choose something you really want, and I'll get it for you in exchange for space in your room?"

"Mammmaa, that's bribery!"

"And if you have friends over, Dewayne can bunk in with Alanna or on the couch."

Smiling encouragingly, I put the question to him. "What do you think?"

"Okay. And I still get to buy something, right?"

"Of course, just say the word."

Arrangements were settled. The children had so much fun running up and down the stairs. They were excited to be there. That first day, I let them have their fun, examining the house from top to bottom. Then I made the inside rule: No running on the stairs. Ever. Not long after moving in, a noisy conversation taking place downstairs caught my attention. Gutsy and smart, having advanced verbal language skills, not hesitating to speak her mind, Alanna always managed to have the last word in any confrontation.

"Alanna, pick your dolls away off the stairway," Ron told her.

"I am playing with them", she replied.

"Not on the stairway. Go upstairs with them", he insisted.

Pouting, Alanna went up to the playroom. Then she came to me.

"Mom", she pouted with a scowl, "can Dad tell me what to do?" She was eight years old at the time.

"Yes, sweetheart. He is your daddy. Both of us can tell you what to do because we both care about your safety. We both love you and will never tell you to anything that will hurt you," I explained to her.

She was all smiles again. "Okay," she said, as she moved on to whatever was next on her play schedule. Ron listened from around the corner. *How did her question make him feel*? I wondered.

In the wintertime, we learned to maneuver the difficulty of getting up from the bottom of the hill to the house. When it snowed, there could be up to twelve inches or more on the ground. The children had so much fun sliding down the steep snow-covered incline of our backyard. They improvised with the lid of garbage can lids until Ron got them a sled. Their Missouri childhoods included snowball fights and building snowmen. When it snowed, we were all ecstatic.

"Mom! Mom!" the children called in unison. "Can we go and play in the snow?"

"Of course," I'd say, "Just be sure to dress warmly and let me check you out beforehand." I would let them play for a while by themselves. Then I would get bundled up and go play in the snow with them, throwing snowballs and sledding down the hill that was our backyard. I hoped they were making some lifelong memories.

The next things on my list included finding a job and creating a social life. No matter how hard the job was, I'd feel more independent and less like an appendage if I worked and had my own money. I was certified as a home economics teacher for grades six through twelve, but home economics teaching jobs were scarce.

Home economics teachers usually stayed on their jobs until retirement. I signed up to be on the substitute teachers list. Getting myself ready for a job at the last moment, while making sure my children were ready to go to their respective schools was challenging. Sometimes, I subbed for the home economics teacher, but most often, I subbed in a variety of subject areas. I did what I could, I worked when I wanted to, and I made my schedule around the children as they developed new interests.

Alanna wanted to ride a bicycle with the other girls in the neighborhood, but she had not learned to ride. She didn't even have a bike. Ron went to the PX and bought her one. He took her to the school parking lot, which was located about two blocks away so she could learn to ride on a level surface. There was no way she could have learned to ride on the steep hill where we lived. After a while, she mastered the bike riding and rode along happily with the other girls her age. Nick still loved playing baseball. We signed him up for a Little League team. He was either at practice or a game two or three times a week while Alanna soon opted for gymnastics. This did not leave much time for me, but I did manage to make some friends. One of them was Rowena, nicknamed Ro. She became, and remains, one of my closest friends. While the children were busy with activities, Ro and I played Scrabble.

My friend, Annette, in Clarksville taught me how to be proficient at making words. Her method of play was intense. I seldom won when playing with her. So, I used her strategies when making words from the random tiles so I could win.

Ron bought two motorcycles. He had also bought a Jeep, from my brother, Ollie. It proved to be useful in the mid-western winters, which were cold and snowy with temperatures delving into high teens to highs of mid-forties. Ron loved to ride his bikes and sometimes I rode with him. I was the worst type of passenger. I needed to be relaxed to lean with the motion of the bike. I just could not get relaxed enough to enjoy it and ran the risk of flipping us over. I did my best, but I still thought it was way too dangerous as a mode of transportation or sport. When he asked me to ride with him, I agreed when it was convenient, with hesitancy. This way, I could improve my riding on the back of a motorcycle and wrap my arms around him while enjoying the ride. I had no desire to learn to drive the other bike, though, and he did not push the issue. I did get my courage up for one memorable trip.

Ron mentioned, looking at his calendar, "I have to go to Springfield for a Shriners meeting. You wanna go with me? We can get a hotel room and stay overnight. Two nights if you want."

Unsure, I responded, "I don't know. What about the kids?"

I wanted a chance to recuperate before the return trip. The meeting was about sixty miles away in Springfield, so I agreed to go. The weather was nice that day, unless you were on the back of a motorcycle. It was early fall. We took to the road, along the hills and curves of the interstate, in the cold and the wind, but we finally made it. I was so cold that I could scarcely enjoy myself for trying to keep my teeth from chattering. I could barely get off the bike. Both of us just laughed as he helped me off. My bottom and my back were so stiff and sore from that ride.

Ron liked to ride his bike to the regular Shriners meetings. He usually chose one of his many friends to ride with him. His favorite riding buddy was his friend, Parks. They often took trips together. Those trips, and the time Ron spent playing cards with friends, took away time from the family. I started to resent that, but I knew the resentment building up was not healthy.

All this time, I worked my home-based sales business. I met many women who were interested in becoming consultants; therefore, I was able to build my own team. I was responsible for keeping the team interested and working. One of the fun things that we did was go on trips to various conferences and conventions the company held.

My team and I drove to Kansas City for motivational training. While women told their success stories, I applauded them with much enthusiasm and some envy. They expounded on what they had traded in for their million dollar businesses. We had an opportunity to sit in the arena with professional make-up artists, models speakers and trainers, decked out in diamonds and furs, enthralled with the choicest tidbits of wisdom being flung out to us, prizes of various gleaming new cars and trucks on the stage behind them. It was invigorating. I had already made this trip once with my leader when we still lived in Kentucky. The trip to Dallas from Fort Leonard Wood was just as fun.

I was traveling with a different team this time, but it was still awesome. The hoopla was an exciting period and the motivational speakers and the winners who were on stage made it seem possible that anyone could make millions of dollars if they just worked hard. I likened it to the annual Grammy Awards. On the awards night, many deserving ladies dressed in their evening-wear finery and walked across the stage to receive their cars and other awards. It was entertaining as well as motivational and informative.

That is probably the reason that I stuck with cosmetic sales for as long as I did. I'd learned so many things through this experience. The lessons helped me later in life when times were tough. In my home sales business, I learned to never give up. It helped me to focus on the values Mama had instilled in me; to focus on hope rather than the negative things in life.

There was not very much happening socially. After soul-searching, I decided to join a group of wives in a group called Eastern Stars, who provided services to the community. Joining the group required studying and practicing; it was very ritualistic. I studied and learned my parts, the secret signals and hand signs, practiced the steps and their routines. I learned the association of the Shriners organization. My husband was a leader in that group. At the end of the qualification period, I was accepted and welcomed into the family of Eastern Stars. We participated in benevolent projects and activities.

Our leaders organized fundraisers so that could give scholarship awards to high school graduating seniors each year. We held activities for children at Halloween and at Christmas with gift giveaways, marched in parades, such as Fourth of July. As individual members of the group, we dedicated time to volunteer work on the military base and in the neighboring communities. The group met socially, regularly, having house parties, and danced at informal barbecues and picnics, playing numerous board games, especially Scrabble, on Saturday nights.

Soon, it was time to leave Fort Wood. We had lived there two years. This time, Ron left first to get housing. I had trouble deciding whether I wanted to leave the country knowing my husband and I were not back to the kind of relationship we had started with, not even after the honeymoon. I wanted the loving, playful moments we used to have. I missed that we did not talk and share at the end of each day. The children and I got ready though, tentatively, to move to the Panama Canal Zone in

Central America. I, again, had to prepare for the movers. Everything had to be clean and organized. Perishable items had to be disposed of. Things no longer needed would be donated to a charity. Winter clothing had to be cleaned and packed carefully for four years' storage. I was relieved knowing the movers would get furniture packed and routed.

I hired a cleaning team to clean the house after we left, but failed the first housing inspection because of some window screens that needed repairing. My time was running out. The housing authority would not schedule a day to fix them within the time frame that I had. So, I fixed them myself, patching the small holes with newly purchased screening and a needle. I passed the inspection. It was time to go.

<u>Another Road Trip</u>

Having passed the housing inspection, I packed ten-days' worth of clothing, loaded the Cadillac for our drive to South Carolina, with a pit stop in Cadiz, for rest and a brief visit with family at Christmas, before leaving the country. I would ship the car, and take a military plane to Panama. It was a lot to coordinate. I was not completely comfortable making such a long trip with just the children and myself on Christmas morning. When we left my mom's house, I drove all day to make the destination point in Charleston, South Carolina. I drove through mountains, tunnels, wind, and rain, through and around cities. Somewhere along the route, I made up my mind that this was the right move to make. If I did not join Ron in Panama, my marriage was over, and we needed to work out our differences. I was prepared to give it one last try.

I had told Ron previously that if I ever left him for whatever reason, I would not be back. So I had to be sure I was doing what was best for all of us. He had left the children and me. All of it was not about the job. He had left me when I was four months pregnant. I resented that and felt the bitterness that we did not work on to resolve. It was the rejection that I felt when I came to visit in Missouri, and he sent me home. It looked like we were the happy couple, but I knew it was not real. I wanted real. I needed to be wherever my husband was to work out those differences. I was willing to drive halfway across the United States to get myself and three children to a country I knew nothing about.

Driving across the country gave me plenty of time to think about it. I had to give it a chance, and that meant Panama.

Chapter 13

TROPICAL LIVING

<u>Panama Canal Zone</u>

We were headed to the tropics! I had wanted to live in Hawaii, but that dream had not materialized. This was not Hawaii, but it was the closest thing to it. Another first: the military hop flight. It took three tries before we finally were able to get a flight. The crew would tell us what time to show up for the flight. Then we had to see if there was space for four more people on the no-frills: no luxury plane. If there were no accommodations for us, we'd take a taxi back to the hotel. I had already shipped the car. On the third call, we were able to fly. The Panama Canal Zone is the isthmus that unites or separates the Atlantic and the Pacific oceans. The country of Panama separates North and South America. Canal Zone was the official name for the U.S. territory in Panama.

The government was run by the Panamanian people as a democracy, but it was owned by the United States. It was not a true democracy.

<u>First Impressions</u>

When we arrived in Panama, we got off the plane directly onto the tarmac. I had deplaned that way in the Bahamas, but was nonetheless surprised. This revealed a lot about where we would be calling home for the next four years. We went through customs without incident and I met my husband and his friend, Percy, on the other side. His friend owned a 1978 Pontiac that had holes in the floor so that you could see directly down to the street.

"Be careful where you put your feet. Those are real holes in the floor," Ron cautioned, with windows down and arm resting on top of door-window frame. They laughed. The amount of exhaust in the car as we rode along was asphyxiating.

"If the exhaust fumes get too bad, put your head out the window," he instructed. Fortunately, we did not have to go too far. It was the kind of car that you saw in Panama all the time. There were four of us crunched up in the back seat. No leaning room to be had. The car had been passed around a few times from servicemen leaving the country to servicemen just beginning their duty. This was the kind of car you saw crowding the city streets. The Panamanians drove fast and with one hand on the horn. This city was always noisy and dangerous.

Our first night in Panama, Ron took us out to eat at an elegant restaurant in the heart of the wealthiest area. The proximity of the oceans offered the richness of the sea when dining out in downtown restaurants. White, linen tablecloths, fancy, heavy silverware, servers in black tuxedos were the norm. Very elegant. I went for the lobster tank and picked out the biggest lobster for my meal. It was served with some vegetables and the best drawn butter. Our view looked out over the lighted city, a great introduction to a country with so many divisions.

There are three parts to Panama City. The old Panama is the one that was burned a century earlier. The ruins and old church and other historic buildings are still near the center of the city. During the day, it is bustling with lots of people an activity. At night, it is quiet and serene. Then, there is the second Panama, Colonial Panama, which has narrow streets, the iron lace balcony, and many historical places to visit. There are many small shops crowded into the space on the street where the merchants half their wares standing on the street side, encouraging buyers to visit their establishment. The modern part of Panama boasts fabulous shopping facilities, swanky hotels, casinos and vibrant and exciting nightlife. The weather is constant at approximately eighty-eight degrees Fahrenheit. Going to the beach was an option every day, especially if you lived on the Pacific Ocean side of the isthmus. Two seasons prevailed: dry and rainy. In the dry season, it never rained. And during the rainy season, it rained daily, real gully washers. There was no in- between.

We lived on the Army military establishment on the Atlantic Ocean, named Fort Clayton. The military bases on the Pacific Ocean side of the country were Fort Sherman and Fort Gulick. There were also bases for the Air Force, Navy, and Marines. All were within the established five-mile radius around the canal, which was famous because huge trade ships could pass through from one ocean to the other. This eliminated 800 miles from the trip and saved much time by shortening the distance to travel around the southern tip of South America. An elaborate system of locks had been created to raise and lower ships up to Gatun Lake, which was eighty-five feet above sea level. Gatun is a man-made lake. Once the ships were through the Canal, the water in the surrounding lake was lowered, thus lowering powerful ships back to sea level. Many ships transported goods, and many were cruise ships. We could stand on the highest point at the lake and watch them pass through. There was barely room to spare for some of the larger cruise ships to get through the canal. We would go and watch and wave to the passengers as they were on decks, yelling, waving, and having a good time.

A Slow-Paced Life

Many things happened during that time with the children. When she was twelve, Alanna fell down the stairs and thought she sprained her ankle. Because it was Christmas, nobody wanted to go to the emergency room. After several hours of trying to convince her that she was not hurt badly, my friend Ro and I drove Alanna to the ER. We were there most of the night because she did have a fractured leg. She was X-rayed and seen by a doctor in record time. The doctors had been extremely busy prior to the time we had gotten there, but then there was a break in activity.

We had shown up during the lag. Perfect timing. We had spent our waiting with Alanna at home, surrounded by family and friends, playing Scrabble, instead of a roomful of sick strangers. However, I still felt badly that I had made her wait, even if she did not complain about the pain.

With three children to raise, I had made several trips to the ER over the years. The X-rays usually showed no breaks or fractures, so most of the trips infringed on valuable time, but necessary to have a medical professional give a negative report than to assume one. Plus, we had to travel across the Bridge of the Americas to get to the ER, and Ro and I had been involved in an accident on that historic bridge. We had sat for a long time on that bridge waiting to get cleared by the Panamanian police after the accident. It was not one of my favorite places to be, and I avoided it as much as possible.

The Panamanians were typically slow-paced, seldom in a hurry to do anything. One time, I came home from work to find a big ugly looking animal clinging to my front door. I did not know what it was. I had never seen anything like it, and I am a country girl. One of the first things they tell you upon arriving in the country is not to pester the wildlife. So, I called animal control. They came out and informed us that it was a slow-moving, hairy, long-haired sloth. They removed it and all those children and adults who were standing around looking at it returned to their own houses.

Our back door opened out so that you could see the jungle, which was fifty feet away. The jungle was densely populated with trees and foliage of every kind. Because it rained so much, the trees were constantly growing. They were so thick that you could not see into the jungle. I never had any desire to find out what was in there, but Nick and his friend, Ferddy, were curious. One day they decided that they would take a trip into the jungle.

I missed him after several hours and wondered, "Why hasn't Nick come home?" It was a rule that I knew where he was, always. I checked with his friends' mothers and confirmed that he and Ferddy were together. They had wandered off into the jungle, thinking that they would be there a few minutes and then come out. But they had gotten lost and could not find their way back. I was right to be worried because so much danger lurked in the jungle. Not just the danger from animals, but also the people who stayed in the jungle and would often prey on others. They would come out of the jungle at night and break into the houses that were situated at the edge. Our house was never broken into, but almost all the neighbors surrounding us were. I hoped they learned a valuable lesson that day. The jungle was not a safe place to be.

Whereas, I never had the aptitude for languages, Nick picked up Spanish quickly and soon was very fluent. He spent much of his time with his Spanish-speaking friends. He also spent time with his friend in the downtown Panama City area. This gave him a chance to interact with the Panamanians.

<u>A Unique Job</u>

Not being prone to just sitting around and doing nothing, I had gotten a part-time job teaching English as a second language. I was a private school teacher for affluent kids who had an abundance of everything. These students were in a Jewish middle school and almost all of them knew some English. The job was informal and the administrators were easygoing. One day, when the class got bored, they broke out all the windows on one side of the room. This incident happened before my shift started. I asked the students who broke the windows and why they did it.

"Oh, it doesn't matter. Our dads will just fix it," one replied.

It was a side of life I had not seen before. I had heard the expression *spoiled rich kids,* but I was seeing them in action. The students seemed to like me, but they did not care much for Americans, in general. The consensus was that Americans were the reason they did not have the best use of their own resources. For example, the best fruit was shipped off to America, and they had to use inferior seconds, in their homes, especially oranges and mangos. When they had a break from their school, they traveled to the United States to attend school for that time or to go on vacation with their parents. If they were going to school, they usually went to a sister school located in Miami.

"Sometimes", students told me, "we go to Egypt, Israel, or Greece for vacation." I often wondered if this might be part of the reason that our American students ranked behind students in other parts of the worlck. These parents made sure their children had year-round schooling. Other nationalities seem to take the education of their children more seriously.

These students let me know regularly that their families had lots of money, yet were not arrogant when talking about the money at their disposal. It was just a matter of fact. They were taught that they could have whatever they wanted. I know this because we had discussions about thoughts for their future. This was so different from the way I had been raised. Education was a serious concept in my family, but it was not easy to obtain it. My parents did not have access to education, not even to the extent that I did. For my generation, the opportunity was there if you wanted an education, but you had to really want it. The idea of privilege, for some, thrives and can be used to make a difference in the world.

The middle school students found ingenious ways to personalize their school uniforms. Only a few things were not regulated, so they were creative. The dress uniform was strictly the same: long black pants for boys, black or plaid pleated skirts for girls, all wore the same white shirts and white socks above the ankle and folded down neatly. Boys wore black neckties and girls wore black string ties. Girls could wear a scrunchy in their hair and earrings, but the size was limited. No large hoops or dangles were permitted. Colorless lip gloss was allowed. Shoes had to be black loafers. All genders could wear a simple watch.

Girls would try to sneak into the classroom wearing high heels, as this was the standard footwear for Panama's women. The students tried to get around these roadblocks as much as possible. Fingernail polish was prohibited, but the girls would sometimes come in with red or pink nails and matching lip colors and be guaranteed them a trip to the administrator's office.

There were all kinds of issues to make the day interesting. I was the only African-American teacher on the staff. I liked the other teachers and we got along. The principal was especially kind to me. On the way to work one day, I had an accident right downtown driving our Cadillac car. A 1979 Cadillac is huge when it is alongside the smaller cars that frequent the crowded downtown streets in Panama City. I was almost at the school when the accident happened. It became more serious because of the language barrier. A Chinese man, driving a small Toyota, and I collided. I needed help and tried to explain to the police officer that I did not speak Spanish, but I spoke enough Spanish to let him know that I worked at the school around the corner. He believed me and called the school. The principal came over to the scene of the accident. It was very confusing because the other guy in the accident spoke Chinese and Spanish. Everybody was speaking at once. I did not cry or get upset.

I called Ron, but he was gone on maneuvers for the day. So, I called Ro's husband, a retired officer. He came right away, speaking to the policeman in fluent Spanish. He also knew people on the police service and was able to ease me out of what could have been a dangerous situation.

For instance, one day, in the cafeteria, we were enjoying lemonade before heading off to the classrooms. The regular English teacher asked me, "What does calico mean?"

With her Spanish accent and pronunciation, I did not know what she was asking.

"Oh! I know", I exclaimed, understanding suddenly dawning on me. The students were reading a story about a calico cat. I explained about the coloration of female cats. Forthright and friendly, all the teachers got a good laugh about this. There was a sense of easiness among us.

Chapter 14

HOME AFFAIRS

Household Help

It was customary to hire help with the housekeeping in Panama. Now, I needed a housekeeper since I was working full-time. It was hard for me to fathom having a housekeeper. I practically used to be one myself back home in Kentucky before leaving Daddy's and Mama's house. But, Dewayne was ready to go to kindergarten, and it became necessary.

I interviewed a few women for the position. She would have to keep the house clean, make sure Dewayne got to the school bus on time, and supervise him until the older children or I arrived home. She would also pick him up at the end of his school day. This was a trial-and-error process.

I hired two different women to work for us at separate times. Advise comes easy with military wives: to be sure to choose someone who was somewhat elderly and not too good looking but would do the work. The idea about being good looking was so your husband did not stray and fool around with her. It was a grossly unfair assumption, I will admit.

The first housekeeper was older, but she was inefficient, and I could not see the effects of her having worked during the day while I was out. After a short trial period, I decided to try someone else. The second choice was a much better one. Her name was Bennie. For one hundred dollars per month, Bennie provided the services we needed. She took care of the house and the children while Ron and I worked. I knew housekeeping services would not continue once we returned to the United States, so I only allowed her to clean the children's rooms once a week. They were required to keep the bed made, clothes hanging in the closet, trash in the trash bin, and the floor cleared. No food was allowed upstairs. Bennie also made dinner, sometimes, for the evening but only when I asked her to do so.

Once or twice each week, Bennie made our food. One of our favorites was Arroz Con Pollo, which is a chicken and rice concoction with tomatoes and green peas. She brought strange looking exotic fruits for us to try. This worked for us the entire time we were in Panama. She became like an extension of our family. I could empathize with her and her situation since I had been in her position when I was a youngster in Kentucky. I made a special effort to be kind and giving. She accepted clothing that my children had outgrown, for her own children. I told her she could sell them if she wanted to. She appeared grateful.

Bennie took the bus into the city every day from the mountainous hills of Panama. When she left her house in the early mornings, she wore the usual dress of the working Panamanians, a dress or skirt and blouse with low-heeled dress shoes. Her hair was always neatly done, and she usually wore a little makeup. Bennie carried her work clothes in a small bag and changed clothes as soon as she arrived at our house. Just before she finished working for the day, she changed back into her day clothes and walked back to the bus to go home.

The men wore a shirt called a guayabera that was made of a lightweight cotton and short sleeves. The shirt extended below the hips and was usually worn with knee-length lightweight cotton pants, buttoned down the front with a collar. It could be very plain or very fancy for dress-up occasions. This was our friend Merv's favorite kind of shirt.

The countryside was filled with people who lived in makeshift houses in the outlying areas surrounding the city. There were many who lived in boxes and cardboard houses that made a city. This was in the poorer part of the city. During the rainy season, the box houses might be flooded and had to be and relocated and rebuilt.

Decision-Making Time

What was not to like about military life? All our needs were met, schools were excellent, my job was a good one and my salary was more than $10,000 than I had made working in Kentucky. I should have been satisfied, but I was not. I was raising three children with an absentee husband. When he was not at work, where was he? Why did he not want to spend time at home? We had everything we wanted, except him. Why? I had done a lot of moving and organizing and making a home for us. I wanted my husband back.

As we sat at the kitchen table, I confessed, "Ron, we need to talk about how you're constantly gone from home and the mess that started in Fort Campbell when you left us."

He said, belligerently, "What are you talking about?"

I told him, "We need to stop punishing each other for things done in the past. I need that for me to continue in this marriage."

I took a deep breath. I had never told Ron what I needed. I started to cry but needed to say these things. I was tired of feeling neglected and abused. Sometimes, I did not feel loved.

Through my tears, I choked the words past the lump in my throat, "I need to feel like you still love me. Do you love me? I need you to spend time with me and the kids. I am sorry if I am no longer the woman you want, but you will have to tell me that. I cannot go on this way. You are always gone, doing who knows what. You don't talk to me! I do not even know what to tell the kids when they ask, 'Mama, where is Daddy?' I think we need to try to start over. Can we start over? Do we love each other enough to start over?"

By this time, I was sobbing uncontrollably. Ron said nothing as seconds stretched into minutes.

He eventually told me, with tears in his eyes, "I don't want you to leave me." He reached across the table to take my hand, "I didn't mean to hurt us. I do love you. Let's start over. I'm sorry."

For a long time, we looked at each other without speaking. I was still crying but trying to be strong. He came to me and put his arms around me. We stayed that way a long time. It felt like confirmation to stay together.

"What do you want me to do now?"

"Cancel the orders and paperwork for the kids and me. We're moving back to Kentucky. I called it in already. I was about to contact the realtor to see when we can move back into the house in Clarksville."

"Don't do that. I will take care of canceling moving orders. You should have hit me over the head with this sooner. I love you. I will always love you. I will never leave you and I don't want you to leave me," he promised. Then we went upstairs.

<u>A Look at the Interior</u>

A group of us including my friend Ro, planned a trip up into the interior of the country, to Costa Rica. We chose to go on the chiva chiva bus like the ones that were often in the city. It was a short bus, about half the size of a regular bus, holding about fifteen people, but often carrying twice that number, painfully lopsided because of the overload. The bus had so many people, often carrying cages of chickens and other small animals—crowded, with many people standing in the aisle through an area that was mountainous, and the foliage dense.

The bus driver drove with a ferocious speed, right along the edge of the road. When I looked out the window, my stomach flip-flopped and nausea set in immediately. It looked like the bus was just going to fall over the side of the mountain. Most of the people on the bus got off before we got close to Costa Rica. Then we were able to get more comfortable. The trip was fun with a lot of laughing and camaraderie. When we got to Costa Rica, we toured the area, did a bit of shopping in the mountain shops, mostly for handmade items, all before we checked into our hotel rooms. We had a wonderful dinner, which included some deliciously prepared lobster and shrimp, as well as plantains and jicama with lots of buttery sauce.

The farmers lived on what they could grow in the fertile land, like vegetables and fruits. The variety of vegetables and fruits was amazing. Some produce was familiar, but there many others that looked foreign. Russet potatoes were one example of the familiar ones. Others included: squash, zucchini, chayote squash, peppers of all kinds, eggplants, tomatoes, mushrooms. All these items were readily available at many roadside stands at unbelievably low prices. The variety of vegetables is also quite a find in the variety of greens, such as lettuces for salads. Their culture is known for its tropical fruits that grow in Central America and other tropical parts of the world.

My friends and I gathered to experiment making concoctions of the various fruits and creating alcoholic drinks to try while we played our word games. There were so many trees fully loaded with fruit, just for the picking, but there were also the tropical versions of others like the sweet potato, called the white sweet potato and the jicama, called Mexican or Chinese turnip or potato. The plantain is hugely popular and plentiful, as well; it became one of our favorites, and delicious when peeled into thin slices, or deep fried for a few seconds. It can be eaten as a snack when cooked this way. The natives who live in the mountainous hills also raise several different farm animals for food.

The Kuna Indians lived in the mountains and lived as they had many decades earlier, according to information found in our booklet about entering Panama. They have their own language, as well, staying to themselves except for the regular trips to the city on business to sell the items they created or for supplies. I recognized them because of their small stature, dark skin, and colorful clothing in bright greens, blues, orange, and reds. The Kuna women wore their mola blouses, gold rings, long skirts, red and yellow beaded headdress, and gold ornaments at neck, arm, and ankle. The method of dress was quite stunning. Their appliqued items have become collectors' items. My friend, Ro, commissioned one of the Kuna Indians tribe when they were in the city, to make a brightly colored panel, similar to a quilt panel, made of a variety of horizontal and vertical lines on a dark background. She gave it to me as a parting gift when I left Panama. I have since had it framed and it hangs on the wall in my home office.

Chapter 15

UNCERTAINTY

<u>Trouble Brewing</u>

As much as I loved the tropics, there was trouble brewing. This was not a good time to be American in Panama. There were some minor incidences that involved the militia, Americans, as well as Panamanian civilians—even though the workers for the American government in Panama were Panamanians, and who made up at least seventy percent of the workforce. By 1988, the people were in opposition to the way the government was being run. I was working in the American government school system and the people who had been there longest, and got involved in the politics, brought in reports of violence and discontent in the city. The unrest escalated. Several events occurred; things that were intimidating and scary. The incidents that happened were classified by the American government. People that I knew personally and some with whom I worked were disappearing because of their politics. Some of them left the country and others just mysteriously disappeared. My husband decided we needed to leave the country in order to be safe. However, it was Nick's last year at Balboa High, and he wanted to graduate with his friends.

The high school was located outside the gates of Fort Clayton, within the five-mile Canal Zone territory. I wanted Nick to graduate with the class he had started with. He had also earned most of the college credits for an Associate's degree at the community college. So, we stayed a few months longer. As soon as Nick finished with school, in the summer, we prepared to leave Central America. One of the teachers I worked with, Ane, had lived in Panama for more than twenty years with her family. She came in to work on morning in distress and looked like she had not slept recently, with dark circles under her puffy eyes.

"Frank (her husband) didn't come home last night," she grieved to a group of concerned, listening teachers. She had already told us that he was involved in trying to oust the present Panamanian President and his political Party. Frank had not shown up for two days. Rumor had it that he had been killed along with some others who were working for their cause. The next day, my friend and co-worker did not come to work. It was unsettling because they just disappeared, and we never heard anything. It was also so mysterious and stressful.

Who was safe? Were we going to have to evacuate? Could we get out in time before the revolt started with the Panamanian people?

No military dependents were allowed outside of the Canal Zone. Other than going to work or to school, the children and I stayed on the base, safe at home for the most part.

We lived in Panama for four years. During that time, we had made one family trip back to the United States, except for the trip Ro and I made to Orlando, Florida, for a week of rest and relaxation. Ron and talked about it before we planned it. He would take care of the children for my trip, with Bennie's help. I felt like I needed to have that vacation time. He agreed, so I made the trip. When I returned, Ron went to Norfolk, Virginia, in May 1986 to meet his brothers, Marion, Julius, and Robert. Julius and his fiancé were getting married. Her name was Niecy; Ron was his best man. He recalls how nervous his brother had been. As the story goes, Julius was about to lose it.

He expressed the frustration he felt. "Man, I'm not sure I can do this. Look at this suit. What color is it anyway?" He pouted as he waited for the service to begin.

"Don't worry, bro, it's going to all right," Ron assured him. "No, look at these shoes. Who wears patent leather shoes?"

"Come on, J. You want a drink?"

"Yeah, but I can't go into the church like that! And look. Just look. I'm even wearing an ugly watch!", he screeched. The music started. Time to enter the church.

"Oh, well," J said. Ron performed his duty, as best man, and was back in Panama three days later.

Chapter 16

LOOKING IN MY MIRROR

<u>Back to Florida</u>

When we moved, this time, we left together. It was the summer of 1988. Ron had orders for a J.R.O.T.C. teaching job in Lakeland Florida, at Florida Southern College. We were still in the tropics. All I knew about Lakeland was what I had read. Ron and I decided to buy another house because this would probably be our last move. Before we left Panama, I solicited a Century 21 realtor to find the perfect house. I gave him specific information about what to look for, as well as what part of town it needed to be. We wanted to be close to the university, an elementary school with a good rating, integrated neighborhood and close to a shopping area. When we got to Lakeland, we immediately started looking at several houses the realtor had found for us. The houses were nice. I realized that I had not told the white realtor that I was Black. I had not even thought it. He showed us a lot of houses, but he did not show us any houses that were in predominately Black neighborhoods. I didn't realize it at the time, but Florida Southern College area was a predominantly white neighborhood that sat at the edge of both neighborhoods.

We had been living in the military and the military way of life for so long that color nor racism was an issue. I think I had forgotten how life as in the south. As we browsed houses in several different parts of Lakeland, I saw two houses that I thought I might like, and they were within our budget. The last house that we looked at sat up on a hill in a quiet neighborhood, with about 40 single family houses. This house set upon the curving street, leading up to a cul-de-sac. There were two other cul-de-sacs in the neighborhood, which I thought would be great for children playing outside.

We walked through the house, out to the porch, and ran across the back toward the lanai. I looked at my husband, and I grinned, saying "This is it!"

The realtor heard me and explained that it was way out of my price point.

I thought, *"But you brought me here anyway."*

The owner of the house, a man of color, was working in the kitchen, which needed a lot of work with the floor being torn up, and the stove was obviously broken.

He said "Well, the house is yours for the price you budgeted for."

"Wow!" I thought, "This is great!" That means he was willing to drop the price about $10,000. The men talked about the house and negotiated further. We were buying our second house—a split floor plan, with the master bedroom and quarters on one side next to the garage and laundry room and the other four bedrooms on the other side, joined with a large family room a fireplace, a large kitchen and nook for breakfast. There was a formal dining room and a formal living room with the entry hallway being about four feet wide. Built with stucco/bricked siding and lots of bay windows, and a window seat on the front of the house. My mind was already visualizing changes I was going to complete to make it ours. I could envision myself curled up on one of the three bay window seats, reading a good novel.

I found a Baptist church in the oldest Black community close by. The neighbors in the neighborhood where we chose to live did not relish the idea that we were Black. In the beginning, we kept to ourselves. In the fall, Dewayne was in elementary school, Alanna was in junior high school, and Nick was in college.

My husband and I, after finalizing paperwork immediately following closing on the house, had decided that a much-needed vacation, without children, was in order. We dropped them off at their grandparents' house, which was something we had not been able to do in a long time, and planned a trip to New Orleans for three days. We were traveling with Ron's brother, Robert, and his wife, Wilma. We made several stops at tourist attractions along the way and enjoyed each other's company. We took a dinner cruise out into the Gulf of Mexico. The air was balmy. Music was loud. Food was excellent. The jokes were entertaining. We had stopped at a Marriott hotel and were relaxing in our room and had snacks and fruit in the car. With some help from the hotel's room service, I was able to create a romantic atmosphere. I spread a red scarf from my suitcase over one of the lamps, placed a large clean white towel in the middle of the king-sized bed. I set bottle of wine and glasses on a tray and put it on the towel for a table mat.

Next, I added crackers and salami from the hotel staff. *"I am glad I brought that bag out of the car"*, I thought. The bag contained fresh fruit and cheese. Last, I set out grapes and strawberries and waited for Ron to come back from being with his brother. I greeted him at the door with a big hug and "Surprise!" I said.

Ron was surprised at my improvised romantic dinner. We had a relaxing time.

When our short vacation was over, it was then time to move into our new home. We had the chore of getting our children registered to their respective schools, and Ron had to leave immediately after we closed, for Fort Knox, Kentucky. Necessary training for his new job was scheduled to last three weeks. Again, the children and I were alone. By this time, I had established a routine. I knew what was expected of me and I knew how to get it done. The children knew what was expected of them, too, so we got along fine.

When Ron first left to go to duty station in Fort Knox, there was news that a rapist was going around in our neighborhood causing havoc. I must admit, I was scared. I was afraid because I was responsible for our children in a neighborhood that did not care anything about us and our safety. I did a lot of praying and a lot of looking out for us; it all worked out. And it wasn't long before Ron was back with us. The primary thing that I had to get settled with the children was to enroll Nick in school as soon as possible. We had his transcript and all the credentials that he needed to begin at Polk Community College, as it was called then. School was just about to start. We only had one car and he had not gotten his driver's license at age sixteen because in Panama you had to be eighteen. I spent a whole day with him at Polk Community College, getting him registered, enrolled, and assigned to classes. He had to complete several tests to determine the level of math he would take to complete his degree. They started at the lowest level of the math classes on the list, so it took a very long time for him to take the placement test for each class.

He had already passed most of the classes for which they were testing him at base levels. We had his report card records, but the official records from the high school and the college in Panama had not arrived yet. Finally, he started going to classes, but I had to drive him to the college each day and then pick him up. It was not long, however, before he was driving, with the license and his own car.

When Ron was home, after being gone for three weeks of training, he told me that Nick could attend classes at Florida Southern College as part of the military arrangement. So, at the beginning of the spring semester, in January 1989, he transferred to Florida Southern College. He completed his Bachelor's degree and graduated when he was twenty. There was no infusion program at Florida Southern. Infusion coordinates diversity in the workplace, aiming for equality. There were only a few students of color and even fewer Black students. There were very few Black instructors, as well. I also enrolled to take a class in children's literature and found this to be so, as I was the only Black student in the daytime class.

Re-living Racism

Moving to Florida felt like 1963, the year I began high school in the integrated system in Cadiz. Dewayne's elementary school had fewer than five children of color of which two were Black I found out later that one of the third-grade teachers was verbally abusing Dewayne, with racial slurs.

"What is a nigger, Mom?" I was shocked as he asked one day when he got home from school and had settled down to have a snack. I did not know about this until much later. He was eight years old and had no malice; he did not know he was being discriminated against. Our neighborhood had the best graded schools in the county, supposedly. Within three years, the makeup of the schools changed. This school would receive students bussed in from a lower income part of town. I was so excited that integration had finally come to our school. A meeting was held for all parents and teachers, old and new, to hear the guest speaker—head of the Sociology Department at Florida Southern College—explain how to relate to and teach Black children. The speaker was excellent, but the audience did not accept his words. The white parents stated they were afraid their children would be beaten up in the restroom, or Black students would bring drugs into the school. All this made me angry. I got involved when I raised my hand to speak to the issue. It was hard speaking to all those white, angry faces, without being judgmental. Of course, they paid me no mind. They moved their children to charter schools and private schools.

I thought that Florida was a state of large cities, catering to tourism, but that was not true. There were some cities, but the state was mostly rural, small towns. A few people welcomed us. We were like fish out of water who had been living in a non-racist country for several years. Florida surprised me. I also did not know how to handle the way people treated us. People told us '*Go back to your side of town.*' The same words I had heard shouted at me when I ventured into white neighborhoods in Cadiz.

One night a carload of students threw eggs at one of the Alanna's friends as he walked home. He was white and upset that other white people were discriminating against him due to his choice of friends. Sometimes, the meanness was subtle; other times, it was forthright. Our neighbors circulated a petition to get us out of the neighborhood. One neighbor chastised my elementary school child for stepping on his grass; not in his yard, but at edge of the street. There was always something. It was obvious that some of the neighbors did not like that we had moved into the neighborhood. But, we were also aware that some of them did like us and went out of their way to welcome us. Racism had not changed in the fifteen years we had last lived in the state. It felt the same. And it hurt just as much.

Another incident happened as Dewayne walked home from school one day. One of the other students' parent accosted him, taunted him, called him some names and went about abusing him in that way. Fortunately, there was an older neighbor who watched the children come home from school and she intervened.

Alanna called me when Dewayne got home. I left work to deal with the problem and spoke with the white woman who had intervened. Then, Dewayne and I went to the school, talked to the principal and had to decide, along with my husband, whether to have him arrested. We decided to complete a police report and leave it alone. My husband, however, insisted on a "prayer meeting" with that father. After the two men talked the next day, that was the end of it.

According to my husband, the abusing father said, "I'm sorry. You have a good boy. I had been drinking. I shouldn't have done it."

"Drinking or not! Don't you ever put your damn hands on my son! Don't you even look at him! And don't you ever bring your boy back to my house to play." I imagine Ron said angrily, all up in the man's face. There was nothing else done or said about the matter.

Dewayne made some friends, but this kid, was not one of them. He became very close with the new friends he made, even to the point that they went away to college together and remain friends today. They are not just the kind of friends that you send a Christmas card to once a year, but the type of friends who have a genuine respect and love for each other and their families. My mother always said that whatever is on the inside of a person is what comes out and is shown to others. Unfortunately, we were adjusting to the ways of Central Florida when things started to go awry with family.

Aging Parents

We were settled and living in Lakeland in August of 1988. Ironically, we had been moving around for almost twenty years and never once got an emergency call to come home for any reason. Then in November, I received a call about my daddy. He was in a coma in a hospital in Nashville. The problem was his infected foot. His doctors in Kentucky had sent him to specialists at Vanderbilt Hospital in Nashville for some special X-rays, which required anesthesia. The doctors did not expect him to come out of the coma and called our family together to say that his body would not last much longer. He passed away about three weeks after I visited him the first time in the hospital.

My mama was devastated, and her health started going downhill soon after. Jean managed her own house and Mama's. At first, this was the way Mama wanted it, but Jean was struggling with the extra work, so Mama hired someone to come in and stay during the daytime and Jean stayed nights. When that did not work anymore, Mama went to live in Live Oak with Neta. She said she was tired of living. She could not walk anymore; her knees were beyond repair. She lamented that all her friends had passed on.

It was almost mid-June the summer of 1990, celebrating Dewayne's tenth birthday with several of the neighborhood boys who were outside, playing kickball, and riding their bicycles. I had called them in for hotdogs we had made on the grill and cake and ice cream. We were just about to wrap it up when the phone rang.

At the other end of the line my sister Jean informed me, "Mama is in the hospital and she is really sick." I felt nauseous. My heart was beating way too fast. I moved into the bedroom, away from the children and sat down. Calming myself, I moved back to the kitchen where the children were seated around the table and started back to work.

While serving the cake and scooping up the ice cream onto paper plates, I asked, "How bad is it?"

She said, "You need to come now."

I told her I would be there as soon as I could get there since I would be driving. I sent the children home with their goodie bags and asked my own children to come sit with me on my bed. I put my arms around them.

"Granny is very sick. We need to go to Cadiz to check on her." I packed a few things for Dewayne and myself. The older children packed on their own.

Nick helped with loading the car. We still had the Cadillac. He left to fill it with gas and had the tires checked while I cleaned up from the party. Ron was in Seattle on a special assignment. I called him and told him that Mama was sick, and we were about to leave to drive to Kentucky.

He said, "You should probably wait until tomorrow morning to leave so you don't have to drive at night. I will meet you there as soon as I can get a flight to Nashville." Ron was right. Night driving was hard for me so I told the children we would leave at first light, next day.

It took sixteen hours to make the drive. The kids behaved well. They slept most of the way. We made several stops so I would not be tired and sore from being in the car. We sang along with the radio, played silly games, and told jokes as I drove. I went straight to the hospital.

Mama smiled weakly when she saw us. We all hugged her. I turned away, with tears in my eyes, not wanting to see her that way. She was receiving oxygen for her breathing. Jean was there in the room with her.

"It's an embolism in her lungs," she told me. "It's the same thing that Grady died from. But he passed away instantly."

Less than a week later, Mama passed away. This did bear down on my heart, but it did not crush me. Although I was very sad, it was as if my parents had waited for me to come home. God gave me a chance to see them, to talk to them, and bask in the presence of family.

Ron's mother and father passed on after we came home also. Ron's oldest brother, Booby, had died one night, while he worked at the factory. Ironically, my daddy's sister, Lily, had been sitting in church when she passed away. When the service ended, she did not move to leave the church building. She had taken her last breath as she sat in church. I was glad we had gotten home in time to savor last moments with our loved ones. These things caused me to spend a lot of time thinking about my morality.

The Next Generations

The children were growing up and making their own way. Nick, having found the love of his life, Tisha, in Dayton, Ohio, married and had one son, Andre. Alanna met Quincy, her husband and soulmate while attending Western Kentucky University, my alma mater. They married and had two children at this time, Phaedra and Phalen. Quinn came along later. One summer, Ron and I took the three oldest grandchildren, then ten, six and five years old, for an extended adventure. We took an airline flight from Orlando, Florida, to Nashville, Tennessee, where we rented a car, toured the Parthenon in Nashville and the Country Music Hotel, the Grand Ole Opry, with the gondola ride through the hotel. The children found that to be unbelievable. Then, we traveled to Memphis and stayed at the Peabody Hotel where the ducks orchestrated a parade through the hotel lobby. The ducks all lined up in a single file and waddled into the elevator. The children and I sat on the floor and waited for the performance. Right on cue, they came. Every day. Applause followed their exit. Another excellent day was spent at the Children's Museum. They played and learned from a multitude of videos, play stations, games, and art participations. We introduced them to jazz as we dined in the evenings. There were so many things to do, and we packed our days and evenings with activities.

A highlight of the trip was the Martin Luther King Monument, the Lorrain Hotel, where he was assassinated. There is an improvisation of a bus ride that could have been any one of the southern states during segregation in the south. My granddaughter, Phaedra, aged six, stepped up on the bus. There were several people (mannequins) on the bus. Some of them were white. The Black passengers sat in the back, even though there were seats available near the front.

The robotic driver moved his head toward her and shouted, unkindly, "Move to the back of the bus!" That scared the child. She immediately turned and ran off the bus and refused to get back on for the rest of the display information. After three days, we drove to Cadiz to visit grandparents. In Cadiz, we stayed at The Land Between the Lakes (TVA created), hiking and playing tennis, the beach, and a rented boat ride. We stayed in a rented cabin high above the lake. It all came to an end with trip back to Nashville to drop off the car and fly home.

When Phaedra was in Girl Scouts, she learned about Juliette Low, founder of the organization.

"Oh, please, Grandpa, will you take me to Savanah to see the Juliette Low House?" She pleaded with Ron.

He asked her, "Who is that?"

Phaedra came back with, "That's the lady who started Girl Scout, Grandpa!" as if he should know.

"When do you need to be there?" We checked with Alanna and made the arrangements for the road trip. Andre and Phalen joined us, as well. We got a hotel room and proceeded to promenade along the wharf, peering into gaily decorated stores for something to buy. Pralines were at the top of my list. We ate dinner and allowed them to get the burgers and fries they wanted. The next day, we walked along the narrow historic streets of Savanah, with Ron pointing out statures and houses and horses pulling carriages. We found the jewel we had come all this way to see, sequestered between two other houses that had also been built around the turn of the eighteenth century, and having green trimming. We bought tickets for the tour. The children marveled at the small rooms and narrow staircase. We took pictures in the backyard and made our exit through the gift shop on the first floor.

Chapter 17

A CAREER MAKEOVER

Starting Over

When we first got to Polk County, I knew I needed to find a job. We had spent all our savings on the move, the vacation, and furnishing the house. I had always wanted to work previously but I had not felt like I had to work. I applied to the school board before we went on vacation to New Orleans and was told there was nothing that I could do since there were no positions for my specialty.

After two weeks, I decided to apply in Tampa, with Hillsborough County. I interviewed with the Superintendent. He hired me on the spot, then sent me over to interview with a principal. I had noticed that there was a significant difference in the rate of pay in Hillsborough and Polk County. I decided not to take the job in Hillsborough County because of the drive from my house and the fact that I had three children to get ready for school each morning. I did take a job with Polk County school board as a substitute teacher for two months. During the time that I was working as a substitute teacher, I interviewed for a regular position as a home economics teacher. The county office personnel told me that my certification was outdated because in the last two months they had changed the rules. My certification was now null and void. To work in Polk County, I would have to take the certification test and the test for home economics. I passed the general test with flying colors. I had not been in school for ten years and it had been twenty years since being in a math class.

There were questions on the math section about concepts I was not even familiar with. The math section caused problems and I had to get a tutor to help. I studied and cried with frustration.

My tutor constantly told me, "You can do this. See, look, you almost have it." With that kind encouragement, I passed all the tests, after three tries. I was able to get certified by the state of Florida in the time that was allotted to me. Polk County then called me for a permanent position at an elementary school. The position was for a resource room teacher in Auburndale Central Elementary. I liked the principal, and I liked the way she explained the day-to-day operation of the school.

The job was like the one I had in Panama, except I had more students. This job was frustrating because of the variety of subject groups scheduled at the same time. There would be, for example, six students who were on third-grade level and another four students reading at second-grade level, and at the same time, there would be two students there for fourth-grade math. Sometimes the groups were larger. Sometimes, more varied. I felt like I was just stuck in this position, not really getting anything accomplished. There were so many students who needed the extra service and just one of me to provide it. I was distraught and frustrated. I was assigned a paraprofessional, who was my teacher aide, expected to assist me with students in the program. That did not work out very well because the teacher's aide was constantly called away from my room to do other things. I stayed at this job until the end of the 1989-90 school year.

I took a job at Southwest Junior High school teaching home economics, as soon as it became available. After I had been at this school for a year or two, the school system switched from a junior high to middle school concept.

The school was for students in sixth through eighth grades. Here, I learned to deal with eleven and twelve-year-old students' raging hormones. It was tough, but we had fun. I taught 170 students each day, forty-five minutes for each period.

There was an overflow of sixth graders. The school needed more elective classes in which to place them. The principal asked the elective teachers to teach an extra class, during their planning because we needed to accommodate all the students. I found out later, the principal was going back on his promise to pay. We were able to work it out and payment was forthcoming, after I had spoken with his superior at the School Board. This principal did not easily forgive me for having called this situation to the attention of his boss at the County office.

My home economics class consisted of topics students would need to know to live on their own and to be responsible for themselves. This included how to make a simple breakfast of oatmeal and fruit. I also taught them how to sew buttons and repair garments using a needle and thread. Amid the poked fingers and buttons placed on upside down, they learned a valuable skill. I taught them how to make chocolate chip cookies from scratch and how to bake them. I taught them the principles of cooking spaghetti and making spaghetti sauce using fresh ingredients. They practiced using microwaves, learned to use a sewing machine to make basic projects, and loved to have something to take home to show to their parents. I felt good about what I was teaching them, and they felt good about applying it.

An Interlude

Off to Bahamas, 1989! The information either came in the mail as a flyer or it was a phone call. We were offered a free trip to Freeport, Bahamas. Completely free! All we had to do was just show up. We made the required reservations on the ship to our destination. The company assured us that all expenses would be paid. We carried the invitation card, the contact information, and our passports.

Ready to have five days of fun, we arrived at port in Miami, Florida on the day that the ship was to sail. This was our first year in Lakeland. Nick was in college, so he was not with us. Ron, Alanna, Dewayne, and I spent the night at a hotel in Miami so that we would be up early for the early sailing of the ship. We got there early and saw people carrying packages, indicating they had been shopping for food, home items, and clothing that we could see. We stood in long check-in lines, just to discover that our names were not on the list. Ron tried to contact our awarding benefactors. They did not answer. This was early pre-cell phone days. Our cell phone was big, bulky, and had poor reception. The attendant had begun a line of those groups of travelers who had reservations made by this company, in another section of the room. We stood in line and waited until it was almost time to board the ship. Ron asked if we should just buy the least expensive tickets and get on the ship.

"We will worry about accommodations when we got there," he assured me.

"Will you take a credit card?" he asked the cashier.

"Yes, of course."

The transaction was completed, and we got on the ship. As it turned out, the ship makes the trip across the Caribbean two times a day, once in the morning and once in the evening. It was like a commuter ship. There were cabins on the ship, but we did not need one as our trip was only going to take about three hours. We sat around the pool or stood around the rail of the ship until we reached Freeport. At the outdoor markets, businessmen and women shouted out their goods, wanting their products to get sold before anyone else's. It was a beautiful, sunny day.

"Oh, look at that!" My children commented on the taxi-cab drivers. "Why are they driving on the wrong side of the road?" The first day that we were there, we were looking for a place to stay. Our benefactors recommended some.

"Yes", they told us, "just keep all receipts and we will reimburse you for all expenses." And they did.

We found a nice efficiency place on a canal that was perfect for us. It had a room for Ron and me and one for Alanna and Dewayne. The next thing we did was rent a car so that we could drive from one end of the island to the other. That evening, just as the sun was going down, we came across a beach area that was completely isolated. It was like we had our own island all to ourselves. That is one of my favorite memories of being at the beach in the Bahamas. We watched the sun set, as the sky went from pastels to deep colors spread across the horizon, sat on the white sandy beach and soaked in the experience.

In the meantime, I had made several friends back home. I met Marilyn at a vocational conference for the County. Margaret was a culinary teacher at one of the local high schools. She became a mentor to me in setting up a classroom restaurant, and a great friend. Annie and I became friends later since we worked with children at our church. We have several things in common, including our March birth-month (Pisces), and same age grandchildren.

I joined a non-profit group that ministered to young people, Progressive Mission and Education Baptist Convention of Florida, Inc. I participated in the annual summer trip as a chaperone, and teacher, as we traveled across, up and down the state of Florida. The convention was held in a different city each year, rotating according to the churches involved and willing to host the group of 500 or more young people. On one such outing, my family was ordering food at a notable fast-food establishment. Alanna ordered water with her meal. The cashier handed her a paper cup so she could get her water at the drink counter. We all found seats and started to eat. Alanna got up from her seat, taking her cup to the drink counter. When she returned, I noticed her cup full of a dark beverage.

"Alanna, didn't you order water?"

"Yes. Mom, I did, but I changed my mind!"

"Did you pay for that mind change?" I asked.

"No, but it doesn't matter. It's just soda."

"True. But unless you pay for it, it's stealing. Take some money from your purse, go pay for your drink. You also have to apologize for taking it without paying."

"Mom, do I have to?"

"Yes, you do. We do not steal."

She looked to her dad, pleading, "Dad, do I have to do this?"

Ron turned to her with sympathy. "Yes, you have to go pay for it, but I will walk over there with you." They walked to the counter together. Alanna did the talking to the amazed cashier.

The trip to the Virgin Islands was like trips we had made to the Bahamas. The Islanders' people are friendly and a lot of fun. Yo, my brother Ballie's daughter, was having a destination wedding in American Virgin Islands. She was marrying Kev, whose family still lived there. An outdoor ceremony was performed with the beautiful blue-green waters of the ocean in the background. With the gentle breeze and surrounding palms and fragrant flowers, memories were made as Yo and Kev repeated their vows to each other. Kev's family were terrific hosts, supplying our anticipated needs. Ron rented a Jeep so we could tour the island and experience the winding and curvaceous mountainous roads. The clear waters and the soft, white sandy beaches convinced me that I need not go home. Duty-free shopping was on my list of things to do but the only thing I bought was a bottle of pineapple wine.

Remembrance

Teaching middle-school home economics was stressful. My supervisor at that time told me about the new high school that was being constructed. When Lake Region High School opened in the fall of 1995, I was one of the privileged teachers to work there under the principalship of Mr. White. I liked teaching high school students this time around, even more than I had any the others. After the first couple of years, I was able to drop the home economics classes to teach only nutrition and culinary classes. I worked hard and felt like the students liked and respected me. It was quite unlike my previous high school teaching experiences. I had grown up and I made the difference. The school itself was built with the exact same floor plan as one of the other schools in the County. I taught there for seventeen years. No two days were ever the same. Every day was a challenge, but this time the students had taught me so much that I became an exceptional teacher.

I checked my mailbox early one morning when I got to work. Inside there was a small note card that said, "Thank you for the work that you do here. You are an excellent teacher. I am glad you are on our team." The message was from the principal. It made me smile for the rest of the week. It is true that a little bit of kindness and encouragement goes a long way.

About twenty years after I had taught at Southwest Middle, I ran into one of those students from my seventh grade class.

Walking up to the counter, "Hello", I said to the attendant at the counter. "I'm looking for something to help keep the bugs off my windshield. Can you help me?" He had a job working in Walmart in the Automotive Department.

"Did you used to work at Southwest Middle?" he asked smiling.

"Yes", I replied. "Were you in one of my classes?"

"Yes ma'am. My name is Jon, he said to me." I'm married now I and have three kids. At least once each week, I make the recipe for spaghetti that I learned to make in your class. My kids really like it. When they get older, I'm going to teach them to make it."

That really made my day.

"What was it that you said you needed?" Jon asked, while I reminisced.

Some years later, after leaving the middle school, another former student, saw me at the post office, near where we were living. I was standing in the line when I heard someone urgently calling my name.

"Mrs. Curlred, is that you?" Practically screaming, this unfamiliar thirty-something-year-old ran over and hugged me.

Perplexed, I backed away. "I guess we know each other! How?"

"Oh, Mrs. Curlred, you're so funny. I'm Andresa. Do you not remember me? I was in your sixth grade home economics class, fourth period at Southwest Middle School."

"All right, but that was a mighty long time ago and you were twelve."

"That was so much fun. You were my favorite teacher!"

After a few minutes of talking to me about her sixth-grade classmates and updating me on how she had become a cosmetologist, she told me that she owned her own business. At that time, I wanted to support her, so I became a client. She's my hair stylist and prides herself on keeping my 'do tight.

Chapter 18

SAYING GOODBYE

In Less Than a Second

Thinking about what can happen in less than a second did not impact me before I imported it to an experience in 1996. It was time to make the monthly trip to the next town to pay the electric bill. They did it every month. Their winter coats were buttoned and zipped carefully. My sister, Jean, and her oldest daughter, Tina, got in the car, quickly, after scraping ice from the windshield. The air was heavy with moisture and clouds were on the horizon.

"Come on, Tina," my sister said to her daughter, "I want to hurry back and see Ann before she leaves." I had traveled to Kentucky with my husband and three children to spend the Christmas holidays.

On December 27th, sitting at Jean's house, I had said to Tina, "Your daughter is getting big. What is she, about ten now? Soon, she will be a teenager. You think you can raise a teenager?" I joked.

"I don't know," she grinned, "but why don't you raise her for me?"

After my laugh fest, I said, "I guess I could. I'm already raising three. One more may not make a big difference."

Less than twenty-four hours later, I was sitting in the living room at Mama's house, visiting with her when a neighbor came over.

"Did you hear about Jean and Tina?" she asked.

"No what happened?"

"They were in a horrible accident out on the Princeton highway. Tina is dead! They found her body lying in a ditch."

"No! You're kidding, right? Please be kidding." My heart was in my throat. "What about Jean?" I croaked. "Where is she?"

"The ambulance took her. She was unconscious. Her body went through the windshield. They found her laying out in the grass and took her from the hospital in Cadiz to the Nashville hospital. She is probably at Vanderbilt.

"Oh no!" I cried, clutching my hands to my chest.

I could hear Mama groan, "Oh Lord, help! Oh Lord. Oh Lord." I told Mama as I ran over to her to hold her in my arms. "I'll go to the hospital to see what is going on. Nick, you stay here with Granny until I get back," I instructed him.

I ran to get into the car with Ron. We could see that the sky was about to open up and downpour. I thought, *What a depressing day to learn about a fatal accident.*

At the hospital, we found Tina lying on the hard, cold table. To me she looked like an angel. That was what I thought when I first saw her. The expression on her face was so peaceful. With tears streaming down my face, I reached out and touched her hard, cold, lifeless body. I felt my heart break. I remembered what Tina had said in our conversation the night before as we had joked about raising her daughter. Were we joking or was it a premonition of something to come? I knew that I needed to go find her daughter to provide what comfort I could.

It was so hard to say goodbye to my sister and her daughter. I spent more than two weeks, in Kentucky and Tennessee, waiting for my sister to wake up. I had stayed with Neta, part of the time, at the Ronald McDonald House. She and I shared a room, to be close by in case Jean needed us. We could eat meals from the well-stocked pantry. There was also a shuttle to take us back and forth to the hospital.

Three weeks later, Jean had not regained consciousness. So sure was I that she would wake up. I was completely devastated. The night before she died, I was talking to her. Her hair was still matted to her head, bloody and dirty. Neta and I called for a nurse.

I asked, "Why has nothing being done about her hair?" Nobody knew but it would be impossible to comb or brush. "Can we cut it off?" I queried.

"We can't, but you can," the nurses told us. Neta and I discussed it and decided to cut her hair. It would be like it was when she was a teenager when she had suffered with a serious dandruff infection. To treat her scalp, the doctor had shaved her head. We did not go to that extreme, but almost. It seemed that Jean released a big sigh when the hair was gone. The nurses came to wash her head. They could not believe what they found. Chunks of glass were imbedded in her bloody skull.

As the nurses picked out the pieces, I hugged Jean and said, "I'm so sorry." That was the last time I saw her breathing. She passed away before daybreak the next day.

Chapter 19

ALL THINGS FUN

Hawaii—All about Perspective

Soon I would be celebrating my sixty-second birthday in Hawaii. I began preparing for the celebration eighteen months prior. I had submitted paperwork to secure the days off from work, completed the application for a new passport, as the older one had expired. The research for accommodations for Ron and me was done. The travel plan determined a route from Tampa, Florida, to Dallas, Texas, to San Francisco, California, to Kauai, Hawaii. There was a quick airplane change in Dallas that connected to San Francisco, where we would spend three days. From there, we'd continue to Kauai.

In 2011, the year of the historic earthquake and tsunami on the coast of Japan, my husband and I set out for Hawaii.

"I'm so excited to get off the ground. This is going to be our best trip yet," I told Ron.

"Well, this is it, so lean back and enjoy yourself."

Neither of us were aware that our travel plans were leading to the devastating tsunami that created havoc on the coasts in Japan, extending as far as to southern California and maybe even Hawaii. We did not know because of the time difference as we flew across the country. It was happening as we traveled.

First, my body was crushed; energy was deserting me. But I had to keep putting one foot in front of the other as we strolled toward the luggage collection floor. It seemed miles away. I thought I was in pretty good physical condition. The second problem was that on the second leg of the flight from Dallas to San Francisco, which was five hours, I got nightmarishly sick. I was sitting in the middle seat on the airplane, next to a young man sitting in the window seat. Suddenly, an acrid taste in my mouth, coupled with a burning sensation and rumbling in my stomach, warned me of what was about to happen.

Feeling light-headed and dizzy, grabbing, onto my husband's arm, I whispered softly, "Honey, I am going to be sick!"

"What do you mean?" he responded. I reached for the little bag in the pocket of the seat in front of me. "Come on. Let's get you to the restroom."

Then, as he watched me quickly sink my face into the little blue bag, he knew. The kind airline attendant helped me through the period of sickness by bringing a cold washcloth and taking away the bag. Holding onto Ron, I made it the restroom to refresh myself. When I got back to my seat, the attendant brought a cup of water and some crackers for me. Through a cloud of gratitude, tinged with embarrassment, I apologized to the young man over by the window.

The cell phone rang at four in the morning, California time. I answered.

"Mrs. Curlred…" It was Shay, one of my students. "Your fourth period wants to know if you are all right because of the weather".

I asked, "Girl, what time is it at your house?"

She chuckled and said, "I'm in your class at school. We are worried that you got caught in the tsunami, so the substitute teacher let me call you. Are you all right?"

"Yes, Miss busy body, we are fine. We only changed planes in Dallas and that had to be quick. We did not know about the storm until we landed here. All is fine here in San Francisco. Now get back to work. I know I left plenty for you all to do. But thanks for being concerned. See you in a few days!"

"Bye Mrs. Curlred!" The class echoed her in the background. That made me feel special.

When we arrived in San Francisco, there was so much devastation from the tsunami. The most important question now was: *Did the tsunami tear up the coast of Hawaii, as well? Should we just spend a few days in San Francisco and then head home*? After checking weather reports and watching the new scene to see what was happening, Ron called a friend that he had in Hawaii to ask what the state of things were. He was told that not much happened in Hawaii and that it was safe to travel. So, we planned to continue the last leg of our journey.

My body energy was still deserting me and I was unexplainably exhausted. I needed to rest so I took a long nap. Ron had rented a car at the airport but did not use it. We had reservations at the Marriott Hotel on Union Square, directly across the street from the Kimpton Sir Francis Drake Hotel, with its iconic doorman in vintage glamor. We had lunch there one day and toured the building.

Our hotel was close to the things we wanted to see, so we set out on foot to find out what mischief we could get into in San Francisco. We had three days to explore. We traveled to Chinatown on the Hop On-Hop Off bus to have an authentic Chinese lunch. For a flat fee, we got to board, then got off while enjoying a first look at the places we might want to visit later. It was a new experience for my husband and me. We had no idea what authentic Chinese food was like or how it was prepared. However, the lesson that we got from our server and preparer was well worth it. Everybody in the place spoke Chinese. That was disadvantage number one. The server pushed a cart to our table that was the cooking vehicle and she cooked and served from that cart-stove. Disadvantage number two was that we did not know what anything was. The only thing we could recognize for sure was rice. Ron and I exchanged several 'what is this' looks. We tried a few things, wanting to be gracious. We had a good time, but left as soon as we could do so without seeming like two foreign boneheads. Once we were back on the street, we laughed and laughed, like silly children.

There was a huge Macy's department store close to the hotel, so we did a little shopping. I had forgotten one of my medications so a trip to Walgreens took care of that. Ron suggested a tour of the city.

"Yes, let's do that from the upper deck of the tour bus," I suggested.

Famous people, monuments and houses used as sets on television shows were all viewed from the tour bus with hilarious explanations. We exclaimed over the beautiful row houses as we rode through Haight-Ashbury, the birthplace of the historic hippie movement. I was too young to be a part of it, but I had seen some of the movies. Our bus stopped on a hill overlooking the Golden Gate Bridge. We asked strangers to take our picture with the bridge as a backdrop. It was just as beautiful as it appeared in print.

From San Francisco, we boarded our plane to Kauai. Ron had called ahead to ask one of his former students if it was safe to come to Hawaii. With the assurance that Hawaii had not been affected, we were now excited to be there.

I refused to let the fatigue and bouts of sweating keep me from having a good time.

Pretty Hawaiian girls saying "Aloha", smiled and offered a Hawaiian lei, a necklace made of fresh flowers, to welcome us. I was sitting outside the airport on a bench while Ron went to claim the rental car we had reserved. I did not tell him how sick I was. The first thing we did was go on a sightseeing tour of the island. That first peek was absolutely breathtaking. The sound of the ocean crashing against the rocks. Palm trees everywhere. It was the paradise I had dreamed about. The mid-March weather felt like springtime in Florida, with a constant temperature of eighty-five degrees.

Curious, the clerk at the hotel asked, "If you live in Florida, why did you come here? You have everything there, good weather, tropical fruits, and places to go..."

Ron said, "Vacationing and seeing different places is what we do." That satisfied her, I think. We located our condo and got checked in. The thing at the top of my agenda was to rest. Jetlag had punished my body when we arrived in San Francisco, and I was still exhausted.

Our quarters consisted of a full living room, a bedroom with a king-sized bed, a washer and dryer, and a small full-sized kitchen. Fortunately, we were on the first floor. I was dragging my body around like a twenty-pound sack of coconuts. My bones had turned into jelly. But, I was in Hawaii and was going to enjoy myself.

On my birthday, Ron took me out to dinner at a first-class restaurant and presented me with a huge variety bouquet of flowers. I had my token glass of red wine with dinner as we sat in lush surroundings enjoying the fact that we could. It has become one of my favorite memories.

As we sat and talked, Ron told me that he had always loved me and always would. I treasure those words, thinking back to a time, when I wondered if I ever would hear them again.

Kauai is known for its flowers. There were flowers everywhere—burst of color here, a kaleidoscope of color across the stream, the yellow hibiscus amid the variations of orchids in hues of orange, purple and pinks hanging onto vines and barks of tees. The botanical gardens displayed their cacao orchards and a multitude of blossoming plants. An abundance of lush fruit trees invited us to pick one. State parks, along the coast display plumeria. And the Bird of Paradise. The land exposed us to so many terrains that I caught my breath with each change from the white sandy beaches to the deep ravines with waterfalls to the rivers just made for kayaking, to the rugged mountains covered in moss. On the beach near our resort was a tree that had been uprooted hundreds of years ago. The weathering had turned the roots a steely gray color. We used the roots and undercarriage of the tree as seats. When we toured the gardens, the potent fragrances invited me stay forever. The beaches at Kauai are white, sandy beaches. Certainly, there were no sand fleas.

We spent one day exploring the island close by. I got involved in a class that was a demonstration of using all the parts of a coconut. The milk, the water, the pulp, and the shell are all useful. We used our rental car to traverse the island from one end to the other, made many stops and were surprised at the variety of lifestyle in the different parts of the island. Not being judgmental, but some neighborhoods were poorer than others. I know this only based on what I saw as we rode around the island. Some homes were in the hills, overlooking crops and farmland; others in the valleys. We visited a former student at his home in the suburbs—an area that had short narrow streets and copycat houses. The sound of the ocean could be heard in the background.

We had gotten tickets for a traditional Luau at a farm that was also a convention center. Beautiful girls greeted us with leis and showed us around the historic Kilohana plantation. There were arts and craft tables with hand-made jewelry and a variety of souvenirs made of grass and coconut shells and seashells. Hula lessons were offered to those not as bashful as Ron and me.

"This is an imu," said the announcer. "See how we put the whole pig in this outdoor oven in the ground? We have added cabbage and seasonings. It is heated with these hot stones. Look at the vegetables (cabbage, squash, seaweed) and fruits on top of the stones. These are for added flavor. This cooks for about eight hours. You will get a chance to try it just before our performance tonight."

Everyone applauded, as he had spoken with such a flourish. Then he said, "You may go to your reserved seats." The unlimited meal was delicious. Not only did we have the under-ground cooked pig, called kalua pork, but chicken also. The pig was served with rice, macaroni, and potato salad. There was poi, made from the taro plant, Kauai's major crop production. This is similar to a white potato, except purple, pounded to a mash and seasoned. Although it tasted like potato, it had a different consistency, when cooked. Another interesting food item was poke, raw fish seasoned with roasted candlenuts, sea salt and seaweed.

"Quite tasty," I said to my table mate. "Reminds me of sushi or ceviche."

Suddenly, the pounding on bongo drums cued the show that was about to start—an exhilarating theatrical performance of 'Luau Kalamaku, A Hawaiian Experience'. It told of a father struggling with decisions about his culture and the envisioned future.

We rose one morning, headed to tour the whole coast. The Na Pali Coast has a tropical rainforest covering most of its surface. The dramatic cliffs and pinnacles along this coast have served as a setting for many Hollywood films. Driving along the coast, we encountered all kinds of terrains. Valleys, gurgling waterfalls, rivers, canals, and fruits. Flowers decorated the landscape. After making several stops along the way, we found an isolated beach which had a picturesque backdrop of mountains.

The Waimea Canyon was beautiful beyond belief. After climbing what seemed like hundreds of steps to get to the top to look down into the Canyon, the only thing I could think of was praising God for the magnificence of His creation. As I looked across the Canyon, I could see deep blue, purple, lavender, orange, and green throughout the environment. The canyon seemed to radiate colors as the sun hit it.

We watched the sun set behind the mountaintops, where browns and golds collided into all the colors of the rainbow. It was as if there was nothing else in the world except the mountains and the valleys below. I lifted my hands in praise. We stayed there for a long time, resting and absorbing the landscape. I will always remember Waimea Canyon as the wonderful place where I communed with God.

The next day we took a short plane ride to Honolulu. The airport and the trip itself were bustling with activity. We waited for a long time because the workers in the tropics traditionally were not in a hurry. In Honolulu, we saw some of the historical sites, like Pearl Harbor, and spent one day at the bombing site. There was so much history to see and hear. It took me back to a time when things might not have been as pleasant. I know it was before my time, but I felt like I could have been there. Videos of devastation showed me how fragile lives are.

Our hotel was one street over from Waikiki Beach. We enjoyed watching the beach goers, swimming, surfing, drinking, splashing, and riding on the waves. There were surfers and skimpy bikinis everywhere. We strolled through the crowded streets and window shopped in the most upscale district.

We stuffed ourselves with a variety of fresh caught lobster and giant shrimp, tropical fruits, and vegetables that were unfamiliar to us before attending the luau. There were many tropical drinks. Time was precious. We packed as many activities as we could into our hours and planned to take a one-mile hike to the top of a mountain in Kauai. We had even started walking short distances every evening to train for this event. The brochure indicated the view from the top of the mountain down into the valley was a must-see. We showed up to join the tour with the rest of the group. It was then that I realized that I had not packed my hiking boots.

The stone steps up the mountain were slippery and covered with moss. And I was having a hard time getting my tennis shoe clad footing on the path. I was also very winded after having gone only a short distance. I continued to climb halfway on the path, and knew I was not going to make it. The higher up we went, the thinner the air got, and the more difficult it was for me to get air in and out of my lungs. I started back down, going backwards. My husband followed me back down the path. We chose to sit on the beach in the morning sun and watch the early morning surfers instead. It seemed that we figured it out at the same time.

Ron chuckled and said, "We should have done this for your fiftieth birthday."

"Probably. Or maybe even the fortieth, but it is still great fun," I told him.

"Let's go somewhere and have a drink!" He reached over and hugged me. So, we just went over to a second-floor bar, sat on the veranda, overlooking the town and quaint little church across the street, and ordered two Mai Tais. We sat there, sipping our drinks and people-watching—dreading the thought of going back to work after a glorious ten-day vacation.

Chapter 20

LIVING BEYOND THE SICKNESS

Something is Wrong

Near the end of my twenty-second-year teaching in Polk County, I felt sick for many consecutive days—lightheaded and nauseated, and my vision was blurred.

"Mrs. Curlred, what are you doing?" Shay asked, as I swatted at imaginary bugs floating in my range of vision. "Don't you see those little gnat-like bugs all around in here?" I said to her. The students thought I had lost my mind.

"No Mrs. Curlred. There are no bugs, and you need to stop," she said.

I often broke out in cold sweats. My upper appendages felt like they dissolved. I had begun to feel uncomfortable in the classroom. It had become so obvious that I was struggling with my health that even the students noticed more often and commented about it. I set up a visit with my oncologist, who was already on standby because for several years, I had an abnormal platelet count with my red blood cells, called thrombocytosis. I was a regular quarterly patient and asked him periodically whether I had cancer.

He assured me with a confident, "No."

But, I knew, even then. My primary care doctor suggested I have my thyroid gland checked. The endocrinologist found that there was a problem with my thyroid. Further examination showed that the thyroid was cancerous. I underwent a series of X-rays, exams, and interviews, then was referred to a surgeon who recommended that the offending gland be removed. The doctors, surgeon, and practically everyone else I knew said that the thyroid issue was not major. Accordingly, it is one of the parts of the body that one can live without.

I had more work and exams done in the Nuclear Medicine department, in preparation for the surgery. After the surgery, iodine radiation was administered orally. Anyone who handled the medication was in full hazmat gear, with gloves, goggles, and the complete covering of the body and head. That was very scary and made me realize the seriousness of the situation.

I consented to the surgery and it was performed at the Lakeland Regional Health Center. Afterwards, I underwent chemotherapy as an outpatient. I went to the clinic weekly for a specified time, started to feel better and went on with my life. Iodine radiation was still required in complete isolation for several days. My husband slept in a separate bedroom. My children alternated helping by bringing meals over when they got off from work. They set their packages just inside the door and I collected them from there. The doctor prescribed a thyroid replacement drug, to be taken every morning for the rest of my life.

I went back to work at the end of my recovery, and of course felt very awkward and uncomfortable facing my students. I was very self-conscious. For two weeks, I wore a scarf tight around my neck to hide the scar from the surgery. I finally got up the nerve to share details. Some students had questions. Others expressed sympathy. A few of the students related stories about their family members who had also been diagnosed with cancer. It was a good lesson for me to just tell the story. The students taught me that.

I continued to work, now without the scarf around my neck. I also continued to have problems. I was examined regularly and at the end of the first year after the thyroidectomy, my examination showed that there were possibly more cancer cells that might have to be removed from the lymph nodes on the left side. The specialist offered two choices: watch the area for four to six months or have them removed right away. This was the fall of 2011. I had planned to work until I was sixty-six years old. However, I had such a difficult time getting back into the groove of teaching every day, that I decided to go ahead and retire; so, in June of 2012 at the age of sixty-three, that is what I did, after teaching for thirty-two years. There was no fanfare or retirement party. I told the administration that because of my health I would not be returning to the school system. Instead, I went out and bought myself a brand-new recliner. Ron was still working. I spent days doing exactly whatever I pleased. Watching old TV shows like 'Matlock' and 'Murder, She Wrote' most days.

The Road Trip

Even though I was not feeling well, we went to New York City because our family had already made plans for our 2012 vacation. I did not want to spoil the vacation for everyone else. We had rooms on the forty-second floor of the Marriott hotel in Manhattan, right in the center of Times Square. The first thing we saw was the Naked Cowboy with his guitar, entertaining a crowd. The grandchildren were embarrassed because he really was naked, except for the G-string he was wearing and the guitar he used to cover the front of his body. We had packed so many things to do in such a short time.

My childhood girlfriend, Carol, who had been a New Yorker for many years, served as our tour guide every day. I had asked her ahead of time.

"I would love to see you guys," she told me. So, the arrangement had been made. From the time we arrived, we were on the move. Carol and I had been friends since before we started elementary school. She showed up on the morning of our second day, hung out with us and took us on guided tours of all the things that we wanted to see.

We saw Central Park in the daytime, as well as at night from a horse-drawn carriage, the Rockefeller Center, the Twin Towers, and the beginnings of the memorial being built on that site. I was humbled as I stood and remembered the lives that had been lost there.

"Wait, Carol, hold up! Slow down," I said to her on the middle of our third day. We were moving at break-neck New Yorker speed, gliding around people, trying not to bump into anyone. Always with gym shoes and a backpack, we covered miles each day. We sometimes separated to do things separately. All of us took the ferry to Staten Island, passing close to the island. We were close enough to take pictures of the beautiful view of the Statue of Liberty and the Brooklyn Bridge. Carol and I went spent one afternoon at an Off-Broadway production. It was a first for me so I was excited to be going. I had gotten tickets for an Angela Lansbury and John Larroquette performance in "Best Man". The performers kept me enthralled from my aisle seats on the fifth row. I did not miss a thing.

The men, Ron and Dewayne, and two grandsons, Quinn and Jayden, visited the Baseball Hall of Fame in Cooperstown, outside New York. My husband was so captivated that they spent the whole day there. We bought two expensive, non-refundable tickets right behind first base for a baseball game at the New York Mets stadium, expecting Ron and the boys would be back at the hotel in time.

Where were they? We waited and waited, and made phone calls.

Dewayne claimed, "We are on our way back." It was almost game time. Another phone call. "Quinn is throwing up in the backseat. We had to stop", he lamented, knowing they wouldn't make it back for the game. In the meantime, with the tickets in hand, Alanna, who hardly knows a baseball from a golf ball, and Jennifer, who goes to a lot of games with Dewayne, took off for the subway to ride to at least see some of the game and the stadium. Fans around the seats applauded as they watched the last forty-five minutes of the game.

So much walking, I thought we should have earned a Walkers' Award, or at least a Certified Amateur New Yorker Award, if there was such a thing. We watched the live filming of the Today Show from in front of the hotel. On the Fourth of July, there was an all-day event with parades and street celebrations, culminating in fireworks display on the Hudson River. I watched from the 42nd floor of our hotel, impressed by throngs of people out to watch the celebration.

The ride on the subway was a novelty for me and was totally insane. There were many people pushing and shoving during rush hours, some peddling video tapes and books. Young men singing and entertaining for tips. Children and grandchildren mastered the subway system and used it as a mode of transportation the whole time we were there. One lesson we learned was that taking two vehicles was asinine because parking was expensive and limited.

We visited Macy's and I was amazed at the size of the store. I believe it was larger than the store in San Francisco. Shopping, however, was not on my agenda so I only bought one or two items. We ate pizza like the New Yorkers: get it on the fly and eat on-the-go. Carol left her home in Brooklyn to come to Manhattan and take us by subway to Harlem. We did a little brand name purse shopping from one of the back rooms that she knew about. When my group came out and were on their way, policemen showed up and arrested the clerk, who had just sold the girls their knock-off purses. Phaedra was traumatized. She will probably never shop again at a backroom back-room shop for cheap deals.

The Cancer Rages

When I went in for my annual evaluation for the thyroid in 2012, the examination showed that there was a possibility of cancer in the lymph nodes on the left side of the neck. This time, I opted for a second opinion and made appointments at the Moffitt Cancer Center in Tampa. The doctors did all the procedural things and discovered that I, indeed, needed to have more surgery to remove some suspicious looking lymph nodes. The surgeon found, during the surgery, one of the eight lymph nodes that he removed was cancerous. I stayed in the hospital overnight and continued the previously prescribed medications.

One day I sat in the clinic while getting hooked up to receive intravenous chemotherapy, and I complained that it was the second time cancer reared its ugly head in my body.

An older man sitting across from me, looked up and said, "You are so lucky. This is my fourth time. Now I have lung cancer."

The man and I talked a little bit about the devastating effects that any kind of cancer has on the body. We discussed the things that the potent drugs do to one's body. We talked about how to deal with the neuropathy, dizziness, pain, and anxiety of having a disease for which there is sometimes no cure. I learned something from that man that day; to be thankful and to feel blessed that you can walk into the Cancer Center and get the treatment that you need to fight another day.

I was given six weeks to recuperate, after which time, I continued to move forward with my life. After the lymph nodes were removed in February 2013, I was invigorated and ready to get back to my normal daily routine. My body was finally my own again. However, the feeling did not last long. I was diagnosed with rheumatoid arthritis and fibromyalgia. Both diseases required some heavy medication to keep them under control. I was also still dealing with the thrombocytosis. My platelet level would range from about 400,000 which is normal, to over 1,000,000. The elevated platelets left me feeling dizzy, lightheaded, and nauseated. Much of the time, I still felt fatigued. And my long bones hurt. Excruciating pain played games along my legs and arm bones, causing me to cry out in agony. The medications kept it at bay, but the had side effects that also left me dizzy, sleepy, and disoriented.

Back on the Road Again

Next on our agenda was an extended trip to Chicago during the summer of 2014. Everyone was going except Nick and his family. They were unable to get the time off from work. I did not want me to be the reason for not going on the trip altogether, even though I did not feel fully recovered. Ron assured me that I could just take it slowly and let my body dictate how much I could do. We drove three cars to Chicago. The trip would be a little different for each family. For example, Alanna and her family would stop and visit friends in Louisville. Dewayne and his family wanted to go to a ballgame before they arrived. Ron and I babysat. We stayed in Chicago for three days doing the regular sightseeing, eating at a variety of restaurants, and taking long walks. We were all impressed with the Magnificent Mile—the stretch of Michigan Avenue from the Chicago River to Lake Shore Drive. We took a walking tour along the Magnificent Mile and the Chicago River trail, boarded a bus to tour the city, skyscrapers, museums, historical statures, and saw many thought-provoking architectural structures.

The Sears Tower, renamed the Willis Tower in 2009 when ownership changed, is one of the skyscrapers in the city. For about 25 years, it was the tallest building in the world. From this building, my family and I examined the iconic views of the city. My group was afraid to take the chance and go up on the observation deck. There were artists and crafts people along the way displaying their items for sale. We visited Grant Park that was established in 1844. It had been called Lake Park but was renamed in 1901 after the American Civil War General and U.S. president, Ulysses S. Grant. Our grandchildren, especially, liked the park, an urban playground that encompasses more than 300 acres and includes an aquarium, planetarium, and Art Institute. It was one of the most stimulating and educational outings that I have ever been on.

While the family was out traveling, we made a stop in Indianapolis for a family reunion at my nephew Chris's house, the oldest son of my brother Tommie. There, we visited with family from four generations. My nieces and nephews do not often get together just for fun and it was a good time. Chris's house was built on a tall hill and the children had foot races up and down to determine who was fastest. There was lots of laughter, squealing, screaming and friendly disagreements as we played softball in the yard. This was hilarious, with the adults creating most of the ruckus.

The family had prepared huge pans of food before we arrived—including barbecue ribs and chicken, creamy potato salad, crispy garden salad, a mustard-turnip-collard green mixture, cooked and perfectly seasoned. The finale was

Tommie's favorite ice cream and a variety of home-style cookies. After all that, we calmed down and sat together as we reminisced with members of our family.

From Indiana, we went to Crossville, Tennessee, to Fairfield Glade, a resort in the mountains of northern Tennessee. It was rugged and deeply ravined in the mountains. We had reserved three two- bedroom condos and divided our group into two teams of very competitive games. One was easy: bowling. Then, we moved on to shuffleboard. Everyone had to play, which resulted in lots of laughter.

One morning we went to the boat dock and rented a flat-bottomed pontoon boat to go out on the glistening lake. Everybody boarded and we motored around, admiring the beautiful homes around the lake. All the children and grandchildren took turns driving the boat.

About halfway out, Ava, my youngest grandchild, squealed, "I want to get in the water!" The water was too cold, even though it was June.

Ron volunteered, "I will go in with you, Ava."

The two of them jumped off into that ice water and started splashing, followed by Jayden and Quinn. We experienced a memorable mountain climb to see waterfalls and to stand at the base of the fall and get soaked, climbing and pointing out wildlife. Everybody was required to bring something unusual to show and tell something about it, like a special leaf or rock. Our schedule was to stay at the resort in Fairfield Glades for seven days, but we only stayed for six because Cynthia, my niece, Neta's only daughter had passed away in Florida. We had known when we left Florida that she was ill, but not to the point of death.

As Ron and I drove out of Florida, I decided we should stop at the hospital, in Gainesville, to check in on Cynthia.

She was hooked up to an oxygen machine, but was still having difficulty breathing.

"Don't you talk, Cynthia," I told her, "Just listen." Her daughter was there with her. We had carried on a lopsided conversation, with me talking and watching the replies she made with her eyes or hand signals. I hugged her and kissed her forehead, saying good-bye to her as we left to continue our extensive vacation. Cynthia had passed away during the night, leaving her five children behind. We cut the trip short so that we could get back and be with my sister, Neta, and the rest of the family during the time of bereavement, staying in north Florida for the funeral. I stayed a week longer to console my oldest sister.

<u>Cancer Again</u>

At the beginning of this ordeal with cancer, I asked my church family to pray that my body would be healed. Yet, the cancer raged on. My pastor, Reverend Jones, was a big help keeping me focused and calm. When we returned from the trip to Chicago, I was in a lot of pain, especially in my hip and knee joints. A little while after, I went to see the rheumatoid arthritis doctor. I was in so much pain that I was begging him to give me an injection of some kind. At that point, I did not even care what the injection was, just that it would stop the pain. Dr. Tal gave me the injection but told me that I needed to have an MRI of my hips to see what was going on. When the results returned, he told me I should see an oncologist as soon as possible. I first tried to schedule with my regular oncologist and found that he had recently retired. The oncologist who replaced him agreed that she would take care of my medical needs and conducted more tests. I was diagnosed with plasmacytoma. She scheduled me for forty-two treatments of radiation. That would have shrunken a tumor in the hip, she insisted.

Again, I decided to seek a second opinion. I was already a patient at the Moffitt Cancer Center, so I sent the results of the MRI over to their treatment and research team. I was told by the head of the research department for bone and blood cancer that plasmacytoma was not totally incorrect, but that my disease was something else. Ron, Alanna, Dewayne, and I were in the doctor's office to receive the diagnosis.

Dewayne said, as we were getting seated and waiting for the doctor to come in, "Mom, I am going to record this meeting…for later." He took out his cell phone and put it on the desk.

At first, the two nurses came into the office. They asked some questions and told us about Dr. Elko's credentials. He was a cancer research physician. Alanna, who had previously worked in a cancer clinic, was familiar with the terminology, so I knew she would ask some pertinent questions. I was diagnosed as having Multiple Myeloma cancer on October 15, 2015. Dr. Elko told us that this cancer was a very rare and aggressive cancer of the blood cells in the bone marrow. There was no cure, he had told us, but it could be controlled, to an extent, and grows quickly if not treated. My husband had difficulty focusing. He asked about practical things like insurance and hospitalization. I could not breathe. Or think. My brain was fuzzy.

Preparation for the surgery started immediately. Every single body system was tested and evaluated. Appointment after appointment. The team examined my body in ways that I did not know existed. There were no red flags. I learned to navigate Moffitt Cancer Center in a new way, exploring areas I had not seen before. The only treatment available at the time would assure a possible two to five years of longevity. That was a stem cell transplant.

Alanna asked the question we all wanted an answer to. She cleared her throat, looked Dr. Elko in the eye, and blurted out, "What is the prognosis without treatment?"

Too bluntly, he replied, "Two to twelve months, in your mother's case, since we are catching it in its early stages." He continued, "We are going to give you all a chance to discuss it and make a decision. Unless you have more questions, we will be outside."

No "call us tomorrow" or "we will call you", was extended. And they were out the door. When that door shut, I flinched. It sounded like a door closing on the rest of my life.

We just looked at each other. Silent and scared. Tears welled up in our eyes, but none were shed.

"I don't think I want to do it," I said, "I really am not sick now. I have a few things going on in my body. This treatment is going to make me sicker." I paused. I was having a difficult time even imagining living every day for the rest of my life, no matter how long, wondering if I would make it to the next day, for two to five years. I could not say that to my family, though. I knew they loved me, and I loved them.

Ron was able to finally move out of shock mode and held me in his arms. As devastated as I was, I felt nothing. I shed no tears that day. I wanted to appear strong and in control. I did not want my family to see how afraid I was. The feelings would come much later. I knew Dewayne and Alanna wanted to cry.

From the safety of my husband's arms, I asked, "What do you guys think I should do?" There was a long pause, but I knew they would be honest with me.

Ron said, "If it means there is a chance you will be with us for longer than twelve months, I think you should go for it."

Alanna added, "Yeah, Mom, they don't always get the numbers right, either. I think you should do it, too."

I knew what Dewayne wanted me to and he just said, "Yeah, Mom."

"Then," I said, "I guess I am going to do this. And y'all will have to help me." I said a prayer as I gave them all a group hug. "Okay, get that team of ours back in here, Dewayne, and let's move on to the next step." I ordered.

Dr. Elko explained the detailed treatment plan. It was complicated even though the cancer was in the early stage. I would have to have a full- time caregiver through my recovery period, which could be as long as one year. My concern was that at this point, other than pain in my joints, occasionally, I was not sick. The treatment that we discussed was going to make me seriously ill, before I was better. And it might not work.

I was glad that my family was with me when I received this diagnosis. Distraught, though calm, they provided the support I needed. I tried to mask my fear and anxiety with confidence as we drove home. I tried to be upbeat and talk about other things. But this dreadful news that we had just adsorbed was heartbreaking. Ron was present, supporting me, for every subsequent appointment and detail, always there, and just as scared as I was.

Thanksgiving dinner was at our house that year. Neta's son and his wife, DeeDee, visited with their family, from Savannah, Georgia.

"Why is she wearing a sling on her left arm?" I asked.

"The pain," she said, "is almost unbearable. This sling helps by keeping the elbow elevated," she explained, then listened to the story of my troubles and subsequent diagnosis as well.

I started intravenous chemotherapy right after Thanksgiving in 2015. Ollie, my brother from Indianapolis, Indiana, came down for the holiday as well. On November 23rd, he said, surprising everyone, "I can go with you for your treatment. Is that all right?" During iodine radiation for the thyroid cancer, I was afraid of the mixture of dangerous drugs going into my body and did not know what to expect.

"Everybody is different," healthcare professionals touted. All the published literature detailed undesirable side effects. But, I had agreed to the treatment, so Ollie drove me to my first chemo treatment. He was interested and watchful. I was scared and learning. The side effects were mild that day and continued to be throughout the duration of treatments.

When she went home, DeeDee had more extensive testing done and was diagnosed with Multiple Myeloma. Her doctors recommended a stem cell transplant. We went through the detailed procedures one week apart, and supported each other as a duo. It was unusual to be dealing with two instances of a very rare cancer in the same family.

After we made the decision to move forward with the transplant, Ron decided to retire from teaching military studies to high school students. He would be my caregiver. I knew he loved that job, the students loved him, and he became a father figure to many.

When we talked about it, I let him know that "I don't want you to give up your job. This will be over soon. We can manage."

Being as serious as I had ever seen him, he responded, "I am going to do this", and set about becoming my full-time companion and nurse. He retired from his teaching position on April 6, 2016.

All my body systems were tested and recorded. It was agreed that I was a good candidate for an autonomous stem cell replacement. This meant that I did not have to have a donor. The doctor would use my own stem cells to replace the ones they removed. The plan was for me to receive high dosage chemotherapy before the transplant. I also had to have Neupogen shots to make sure that the cells did not clump together when they were removed.

I had to always be within forty-five minutes of the hospital, once the treatment began. So, my husband and I moved into a hotel suite in Tampa. I got up and got dressed every morning and he drove me to the clinic for whatever procedure had to be done that day.

One week before the transplant, my bone marrow was extracted and the machine separated my blood into its parts: the platelets, the stem cells, and white blood cells. A machine destroyed the damaged stem cells and cleaned up the platelets. Then, stem cells were examined, cleaned, and stored; others were frozen. The frozen stem cells would be used later if a second transplant was needed. Blood was replaced in my body. During that time, I had no immune system. Because the white blood cells are the defensive cells that protect the body from infections, I was very susceptible to all diseases, bacteria, and viruses. I had to be incredibly careful. My family could not visit.

Then, the doctors gave me a heavy dose of chemo that made me extremely sick, with nausea, loose bowels, headache, and fatigue. At the end of a week of monitoring and receiving a variety of medical procedures, it was time to conduct the transplant. They started the procedure as scheduled but it had to be rescheduled because the Neupogen shots were not doing their job to get the stem cells ready for extraction.

On May 4, 2016, the harvesting of the stem cells was complete. On the tenth, the high dosage chemo was administered. This was to destroy any remaining damaged cells in my body. The next day was a day of complete rest. Then, on the May 12th, which I designated as my second birthday, the transplant was complete. The doctor replaced the white blood cells that had been removed from my body, which gave my body a chance to start producing new stem cells that were not damaged by cancer. I became exhaustingly sick, with nausea, no appetite, diarrhea, muscle fatigue, and bone pain. My body felt bruised and abused. I stayed at the Moffitt clinic until I gathered enough strength to depart. Ron took me back to the hotel suite late in the evening to recuperate. He did not leave my side, except to go downstairs to escort Pastor Jones up my cubicle, right in the middle of my gagging and being incapacitated. Fatigue, like no other symptom I had, left me feeling tired out and dreadfully weak.

Ron struggled to find things to make or food that I would eat. He was keeping a record on how much water I drank, how much food I ate, how many times I went to the bathroom, how many hours I slept, how many times I got up in the middle of the night, and how many times I complained about pain. I was trying to drink at least ninety-six ounces of water each day. My usual exercise was to get out of the car when returning from the treatment center and walk around the parking lot as many times as I could. Physical therapy was an option for me, but I did not choose it. I also was offered a nutrition plan, social and psychological services, along with support groups. If I felt like I needed one of the services, then I asked for it and it was scheduled. I used social services and the nutrition plans the most.

I was released from the hospital outpatient clinic in the middle of June and was so glad to get home to sleep in my own bed with my personal belongings around me. Ron continued as my caregiver. This could not have been easy for him simply because this was not his skillset. I knew he could not cook, because he had no interest in cooking. He had never cooked anything. His career in the military had been as an infantry soldier. If he got hungry, he took a can of something, most likely beans, out of the ever-present rucksack on his back, opened it and proceeded to eat. Every morning, Ron made sure I got up and got dressed. No sloughing around all day in pajamas. He made breakfast, put it on the table and called for me to come and eat. My box of medications was placed on the table nearby. The meals in the mornings were simple: toast and applesauce with bacon or a smoothie made from fresh fruits. And there was always freshly brewed coffee.

Sometimes, Ron would ask Alanna to bring a plate of whatever she made for her family's dinner. He prepped salads and cooked on the grill for evening meals. I would sit in the backyard and watch with him with amazement as he smoked chicken or pork. As I look back on it, he did an awesome job of taking care of me, even after he was diagnosed with prostate cancer. Ron was sick too, but he kept it from me and never faltered in his care-taking skills. There were no complaints, not once, about the prostate cancer that wrecked his own body. He endured his forty-two radiation treatments, downplaying the side effects, driving himself to the other side of town and back for those treatments, in good spirits and joking with nurses. They told me how he brought them doughnuts to their stations. Then, he would come home to check on me to be sure my needs were met and collapse in the recliner to sleep for three or four hours. Upon awakening, he still would not let me do anything for myself.

As he struggled to regain his strength, Ron continued to keep the kitchen spotless, did our laundry and housekeeping like he had been doing it his whole life. Since our time in Panama, our marriage relationship had blossomed and we moved forward in trust and love. Not a day goes by that I do not express love and kindness and gratitude for our journey together.

Although I was prescribed a variety of medications, the most important ones, I suppose, were the ones just for the maintenance of the disease. These were chemotherapy in the form of a capsules. My oncologist told me there were only a few drugs that had been developed to treat this disease. I tried two medications and used them for a while. Then, I switched to two more of the drugs that seemed to work well together. I started with a drug called Revlimid. Later, I moved onto Ninlaro and Pomalyst, which were taken together. There were specific instructions associated with when to take them and how to take them, also wellness and maintenance care which included monthly blood checks with oncology and regular checkups with the primary care doctor. I was prescribed several supplements, such as multiple vitamins, fish oil, calcium, Vitamin D, and a daily aspirin. There are so few drugs for the treatment of Multiple Myeloma, that the available drugs are prescribed and when they no longer work, the other drugs are prescribed thereafter. I am supposing that one could go on a never-ending cycle of using the available ones.

<u>Staying Healthy</u>

For me, this is retirement. Every day that I live, I am grateful. I give thanks to God for allowing this body to live on. I am thankful that He allows His spirit, the Holy Spirit, to live in this wreck of a body. I am grateful for small things like the birds singing and the change in the temperatures, friends, good neighbors, children who come back to check on me, and grandchildren who love me and show their love in many ways. I love going to the public celebrations that the American Cancer Society promotes to celebrate people who have this dreadful cancer and who continue to fight it. I have learned that every day is a gift. I listen for birds' songs in the early mornings as I get up each morning and unwrap my gift of life to see how many things I can plug into the day that might help someone else. I have been a school volunteer, reading to students who are behind in their studies. I played Scrabble at the Rehabilitation Center. I wrote and mailed greeting cards for my retired teachers' group.

How can I be a positive influence on someone else's life? That is a question I seek to answer daily.

After the success of the stem cell transplant, I was assigned a new team of doctors for the maintenance of the disease. I also elected to have one oncologist. So, all my needs are taken care of by Dr. Shain, hematologist-oncologist at Moffitt Cancer Center in Tampa, Florida. When we first met, he drew pictures to explain the processes and techniques. He made notes for me and asked if I understood. He still does that when I see him. Living with cancer requires a positive attitude about life. It is also important that one eats properly and regularly. Good nutrition is a must. It is not about the weight that one carries on his or her body, but more about the nutrition that enters to fight the disease. Dr. Shain tells me to eat what I want but to be reasonable with the amount, and not to be so concerned about how much I weigh. He tells me to do the things I want to do and to enjoy my life. I think that is good advice. I make the effort to do so every day.

I like my oncologist very much. Dr. Shain is personable, kind, and knowledgeable. He monitors my health and keeps tabs on those he supervises. He listens to me and bases my treatment on the symptoms I tell him I am experiencing, as well as what the results of blood work and other tests show. He gives me the facts and tells me what the options are.

Then he asks, "What are we going to do?" I appreciate this attitude that allows me to actively participate in my treatment plan. The team working with him, that has been assembled for my care, is also attentive and efficient.

"Dr. Shain, my husband and I are planning a cruise to Alaska. Do you think it's okay to go?" I asked at the end of a recent visit.

"Oh, that sounds like fun. When will you go?"

I explained it was still six months off.

"Of course, do it!" he said enthusiastically. "Go! We will see how you are doing on your meds when it's closer to your travel date. Maybe we can give you a vacation from the chemo while you are on vacation. My sister lives in Alaska. I fly up to see her often. I know you will have a good time."

Retirement

Some people say retirement is boring. They believe there is nothing to do. After I recovered some of my health, I felt like I needed to be doing something to give back to others. I signed on to a group that was called Reading Pals, set up by the benevolent group, United Way, to go to various elementary schools and read to kindergarten students who were having trouble with literacy. Many times, these students had difficulty staying on task with the teacher.

When I visited, I sat at the kindergarten-sized table and the teacher dismissed the selected three students. They came to the table beaming and hugging me.

I posed icebreakers like, "What did you do after school yesterday?" Then, introduced the story of the day, showing them the book cover. I would question to see if they could relate the characters. After the discussion and introduction, I read to the story to the students, pausing to show pictures and discuss words. Afterward, I asked pertinent questions about the story. This helped students to focus on things like setting, place, time and to be able to understand the context better. I worked at three different schools during the time in which I volunteered. The same book was read each week at each of the schools. One of our favorites was The Relatives Came, Story by Cynthia Rylant; Illustrated by Stephen Gammell. We started with the cover and talked about the car the relatives traveled in, a station wagon.

I worked two days each week. Sometimes, I volunteered to do other jobs at the school if I was needed. After three years, I was ready to move on to do something else. There was work to be done and I had more projects in mind. I moved on to the next thing and took up gardening. It has been very good for me to be outside and play in the dirt, calm on my hands and knees, trying to create something; trying to make something grow. Ron helped me dig up the backyard. At first, I just tried planting herbs, such as basil, sage, oregano, mint and rosemary. My first harvesting brought so much produce that I had trouble deciding what to do with it. The plants were beautiful, so healthy looking and fragrant. I loved being outside, as I did while growing up, digging, and playing in the dirt. So, I had the grandchildren come over, put the produce in sandwich bags and delivered them to all the neighbors. During a harvesting season, I grew greens: collard greens, mustard greens, and turnip greens, tomatoes, yellow crookneck squash, bell peppers, in a variety of colors, and jalapeno peppers. I used what we could use and gave the rest away. Then I decided, at the urging of my grandson, Phalen, who is a plant specialist, to plant and grow a variety of lettuce. The harvest was plentiful.

My sister is a community health specialist and a preacher who conducts classes about mental and physical health. I am a member of her ministry team and I am also a community health worker. I went to one of her meetings and took a basket of the lettuces that I had grown and gave them away to the senior citizens. They were glad to be gifted with fresh greenery, and you can just imagine the salad they would have made on your plate. Doing this made me feel especially good.

Twice, I have spoken about the very rare cancer that I have in my body. The first time, I spoke to a group of young people to encourage them to always persevere and never ever give up, no matter what the problem is. God will provide what is needed. It was a very impromptu presentation. I was not on the program to speak that day and was officiating something else. Suddenly, I felt the urge to tell my story. Maybe one of the 500 young people sitting in front of me needed a little nudge of hope. I recognized the common feeling of desperation and hopelessness.

This was a Christian children and youth conference, under the direction of the Reverend Brown, Director of the Mission and Education state Baptist Convention of Florida, Inc. Reverend Brown is also Pastor of Greater Mount Vernon Missionary Baptist Church in Jacksonville. I have been working with this group of young people and adults for more than 26 years, witnessed the development of the program and watched this week of summer camp enhance and even change some of their lives dramatically.

Reverend Brown said, when asked if I could include this work in my repertoire, "Of course! Mrs. Curlred has had a substantial influence on the children and youth auxiliary in our state for more than two decades. She has been effective in her leadership positions and has brought much insight to the development of the curriculum. She has brought encouragement, leadership, discipline, and fun to the young people as she watched their progress and development. It is evident that her work has been fruitful in the enthusiasm and anticipation that they show to commit to attending year after year."

The second presentation was at the request of Reverend Izora, my youngest sister, who asked me to be the keynote speaker to a group of cancer care workers she trained and certified to be volunteers in the community, as part of the Community Health Workers and Project HOPE, in Atlanta, Georgia. I am a Volunteer Community Care Worker. This particular effort was coordinated with the American Red Cross. I work with Reverend Izora, on the board of an organization called Life Limbs, Inc. (founded by her and her husband) which is a nonprofit organization that ministers to women and to those who are homeless and near-homeless, or otherwise need some assistance. There are several things that we do during the course of a year and classes that she presents. I assist her in the presentations as she teaches about chronic illnesses and how to control them. An example of this is the classes on controlling diabetes, for those diagnosed as diabetic or borderline. Also, the perfect platform for me to explain Multiple Myeloma, a terminal cancer, and the devastating effects it can have on the affected patient and family members; an opportunity for me to tell my story of survival.

Retirement has indeed awakened new desires. My husband and I decided a long while ago that we wanted to visit all the states in the country, not only to pass through, but to also spend time. We still have not seen the seven states up on the Eastern Seaboard. We have more traveling to do and more stories to write. Much has been left out in this telling, so I will add those things to my to-do list for the future.

A Dual Celebration

As I leaned in to take a look back into the past, celebrating my 70th birthday became important to me. Cancer has not won. I wanted to celebrate that and my birthday.

"Alanna, will you and the family put together a birthday celebration for me?" I asked my daughter.

"Yeah, Mom, we will do it. Just get me the guest list and tell me when."

I began to look forward to the day with great anticipation.

On the weekend long party, I greeted people who were part of my past, as well as my family from Kentucky, Ohio, Indianapolis, Georgia, and New York. My church family was in attendance, as well. We spent an afternoon in St. Pete at the beach (one of my favorite things to do). We all trooped into my home church for morning service on Sunday. I was overjoyed, to say the least. What an awesome time we had at the Cleveland Heights Country Club. I was surprised to see that some of my former co-workers were there. Everyone who spoke said wonderful things about me. I cried tears of appreciation and love as I listened. Old friends and new friends were there, just for me. My husband, children, grandchildren and great granddaughter were proud to be with me on the dance floor as we danced to the music—a memory that I cherish.

An elegant meal of fish, pork, green beans, potatoes, rice, with large shrimp and fruit and cheese as appetizers, was served, and the finale of birthday cake. We danced to gospel music, while Nick filled the role of comedian, disc jockey and master of ceremony. More than one hundred people helped me celebrate my life. My granddaughter, Phaedra, was away at school and could not attend, but she created a special gift for me, an original dedication poem:

Back in My Body (For Grandma)

And one day there will come a time
when 700 is the new 70
and 70 is the new 7.
there are not enough years
for all the joy left in me,
all the smiles, sweat, and sweet tea,
I frolic in Seattle meadows
and there are no bones that wail in pain
I am young, unstoppable,
and I leave my mouth open
while it fills with rainwater,
dancing feels different
when you are untroubled,
diving into the reckless sea.
to be young is to be carefree,
once I jumped off the cliff of uncertainty
and didn't think of the consequences:
felt nothing on the way down,
laughed with my fractured bones,
even now despite living in a world,
that beats at my skin, and causes aches in my joints
I have forgotten as the years passed,
I still laugh as my beating, thumping, breathing bones
continue to dance like hurt is an unknown word.
this body is mine and I will hold hands with myself,
frolic in meadows of countries and states
I have not been in yet, for eternity.
This body of mine is infinite.

REFLECTIONS

My Story

My life has been a time for love and forgiveness, a time for travel and a time for being at home; a time for raising a family, and a time for saying goodbye; a time for helping others, and a time to accept help. Mostly, it has been a time for sharing what God has given me through the experiences I survived. That started with my mom and dad, who they were and what they gave me: values and determination to be successful. But still, I had not anticipated the remarkable life that God planned for me. I did not begin my journey with many physical things, but I always knew I was loved by my family. The times did not love me and tried to keep down.

I am proud of my accomplishments and the accomplishments of my husband and my children; I know they will do well as they continue to work in their chosen professions. I am proud of Ron and what he accomplished during his military career. He surprised us all by finishing his Bachelor's degree. After retiring from the military, he chose to go into the teaching profession along with the most of his family, and retired after twenty-three years of service. I am grateful that we have had a good life and do not take anything for granted.

I reflect back on what Mama said about being proud of who you are and what you have. I am a product of all those with whom I have come into contact over the years. It is God's goodness that allows us to do with it as we will.

Several years ago, I was able to make peace with who my dad was, and the role that he played in my life. I was able to forgive him for the wrongs I perceived him having done to me and to our family. At that time, I was also able to forgive myself for the feelings that I harbored all those years. He was sick and needed our help. I was too young and too immature to recognize that. I know that Mama forgave me for many things that I did, knowing she would not have approved.

It has been said that these are my 'Golden Years'. For a while, I wondered how they could be considered special with all the struggles that I endure. I have come to see that it is the struggles in life that made me strong. I hope the things I have experienced are worthy lessons, a legacy, so to speak, for my children. My husband and I have shown them that they can accomplish whatever is in their hearts. We have tried to model that for them, teaching them, as they lived in different parts of the world, that all people are the same—and to see beyond the exterior of the color of a person's skin. As I am moving toward my 'Golden Years', it is my goal to continue to be healthy, to be happy, to prosper, and to show love for others. I believe Mama would be proud of me. I know she always knew how much I loved her. She used to tell me that God gave me a special gift. Now I think I know what the gift is.

This is truly the story of a little girl who had to face many obstacles. For each day, for each year, and for each moment that I continue to breathe, I am thankful. Hopefully, I am not the same little girl that I was in the early 1950s. The racism continues in this country and I am disheartened to see how it is still affecting our generations. I have done a lot of things, been a lot of places, witnessed things I did not think I would ever see, tasted foods when I did not know what they were, and now, I have learned to be still and enjoy what God has placed in front of me.

What will I do now? Where will I go from here? I look forward to each challenge. This prayer represents all that I have overcome. I pen these words for my children, so they will always know the supreme power of God:

Heavenly God,
my provider, my heavenly father, my keeper
my heavenly father, my friend
my strength in weakness
my strong tower
all to which I run in my times of need!

Precious Lord, you are faithful, but I sometimes lose my way.
Precious Lord, you are blameless,
while I am a reformed Sinner.
Precious Lord, you are strong when I am weak.
Precious Lord, you are a healer and hold all manners
of sickness at bay.
Precious Lord, you walk and talk with me,
as I try to focus on your word and listen.
The God of my salvation, I call on you, and you are here.
Thank you, my Heavenly Father, my Precious Lord, for
healing me over and over.
Thank you for giving your perfect son on my behalf.
Thank you that you allow us, through His blood,
to become heirs with Him in eternity
I petition these words to you and celebrate your gift of life.
I pray that they will be received in the spirit
that they are written.

Amen.